SECRETS OF
Lawyer Video
Marketing
IN THE
AGE OF

Throughout this book you'll notice a square bar code called a QR code (quick response code). Use your smart phone to scan the QR code. Doing that will take you to the video Gerry is talking about. You need a free app that allows you to scan this code. If you don't have this free app on your phone, go to the app store and search "QR Reader" and download a free QR reader to your smartphone.

SECRETS OF
Lawyer Video Marketing
IN THE AGE OF You Tube

GERRY OGINSKI

WORD ASSOCIATION PUBLISHERS
www.wordassociation.com
1.800.827.7903

Designed and published by

Word Association Publishers
205 Fifth Avenue
Tarentum, Pennsylvania 15084

www.wordassociation.com
1.800.827.7903

There are few people in this world who can multitask and accomplish great things. One them, and the greatest person in my life is my wife, Wendy. She has enabled me and encouraged me with all that I do. She is the center of my universe. My four fantastic kids, Joseph, Shari, Mia & David are my guiding light that propels me to new heights in my career as an attorney and video marketer and most importantly, as a father.

I want to thank my business partner, Harry Brockman for his guidance, wisdom and experience in TV and video along with his wonderful and brilliant wife Kathleen (my production manager). Much gratitude goes to Joe Kalange for his technical expertise in making our video magic happen behind the scenes.

I want to thank Fairfax, Virginia personal injury attorney Ben Glass for getting me started on the road to education-based marketing so many years ago. Finally, I want to thank my mentor Kevin Nations on teaching me incredible new ways to understand the transformational value of what you have to offer others.

Thank you all. You are truly inspirations in my life.

Gerry

TABLE OF CONTENTS

Chapter 1 - I'm a Lawyer, Just Like You 9

Chapter 2 - A Budding Video Producer 19

Chapter 3 - The Worst Marketing Advice I
Ever Received: "Get Your Name Out There". 29

Chapter 4 - How Are You Different? 43

Chapter 5 - A Revolutionary Idea. 57

Chapter 6 - Sharing the Vision. 67

Chapter 7 - How to Convert a Viewer into a Caller 77

Chapter 8 - Video Is a Portal 93

Chapter 9 - Quality Counts. 111

Chapter 10 - Seven Reasons Not to Create Video 121

Chapter 11 - You Must Understand Your Viewer 131

Chapter 12 - Do or Die .143

Chapter 13 - How Not to Create Attorney Video 151

Chapter 14 - Even More Things You Should
Never Do with Video. 165

Chapter 15 - Two Things Never to Talk About on Video .179

Chapter 16 - You Can Do This Too 187

Chapter 17 - Don't Believe the Hype; Your
Video Equipment Is Meaningless 203

Chapter 18 - Step-by-Step Video Guide 211

Chapter 19 - Step Away from the Wall and
Turn On Your Lights 225

Chapter 20 - Why You Need to Shoot Video
in Your Office. 233

Chapter 21 - Most Video Production
Companies Can't Help You. 241

Chapter 22 - Important Tips You Need to Know 249

Chapter 23 - Video Marketing for Lawyers 261

Chapter 24 - See What Your Fellow Lawyers
Have to Say About Gerry 265

Chapter 25 - Now Why Would You Want to
Create Video?. 287

Chapter 26 - You've Reached the End... But
Your Journey Just Begins. 293

Chapter 27 - Learn About Gerry 297

I'm a Lawyer, Just Like You

A BEHIND-THE-SCENES STORY OF AN EXPERIENCED ATTORNEY WHO LEARNED HOW TO MARKET HIS SOLO LAW FIRM WITH GREAT SUCCESS

You're stressed. Dealing with clients all day is exhausting. Being on the phone and having to put out legal fires is tiring. Dealing with obnoxious adversaries is annoying. Handling disagreeable clients is part of your job. It's all part of being a lawyer. I know. I'm a lawyer. A medical malpractice lawyer. A trial lawyer. I practice in one of the most competitive legal markets in the country, New York. I know exactly what you deal with. I've been doing it for more than 23 years.

I know many lawyers who complain that they can't stand the practice of law. They bitch and moan while sitting in the lawyer's lounge in court or while waiting for their case to be called in a jam-packed courtroom with 100 other lawyers. They complain that their workload is overwhelming, their clients are demanding, and the number of new clients is dwindling daily.

These same lawyers claim that their current advertising and marketing is not producing the same number and quality of cases that it used to just a few years ago. They agonize about how much it costs for a full page ad in the yellow pages and whether it's still worth it. Their referrals are down, and the firm is having cash-flow problems. Layoffs are in the foreseeable future if things don't improve. I sympathize with these lawyers, but I don't feel bad for them.

Why not? Because I was in their shoes.

AN EXPERIENCED ATTORNEY GOES OUT ON HIS OWN

I was a struggling solo practitioner who had left the comfort of my large law firm to open my own practice. I had taken all my cases with me when I decided to start my very own law firm. That worked well for two years. I thought that since I was well known in my legal community that the cases would automatically flow into my new office because of who I was and my prior experience getting results for my medical malpractice and personal injury clients. Hah! Although I was very experienced as an attorney, I was green and wet behind the ears from a business standpoint.

I had done everything right. I found an inexpensive office. My overhead was low. I had a nice caseload. I had a bank willing to work with a new law firm if cash flow got rough. Then when my cases started to settle and get resolved by going to trial, I'd return back to the office wondering why I was not replenishing my caseload with new cases to take the place of ones I had just resolved.

That's when I would stare at the phone, literally, wondering when and if it would ring. I started getting worried when my secretary would remind me that my cases were dwindling and I needed to do *something* to generate more cases. The calls were not happening. I started to panic. I began looking at what other lawyers were doing to generate cases in their office. I mistakenly assumed that the advertising other lawyers in my field were using were working and cost-effective. "If it's working for the biggest lawyers in my town, then it must work," was my thinking.

THE WRONG MINDSET

I started with display ads in promotional books. Then went to classifieds in my local newspaper. I called the yellow pages rep, believing that if I created an ad just like the other lawyers had, then surely I would get *some* calls.

Day by day I was getting more and more desperate for ways to make the phone ring. My cash flow was trickling and I had expenses. I had to pay the rent, pay my secretary, pay my vendors, and still take home a paycheck. The yellow pages rep told me that they would design my ad and I'd "love it." Hah. Little did I know that they designed all the ads and there was no way to distinguish one lawyer from another.

I tried every method of attorney advertising except for bill-boards. I even did a TV commercial. I will tell you that of all my marketing, my yellow pages ad was the most expensive. It also had the worst ROI (return on investment). Each of the methods I used did generate one or two clients that would pay for the cost of the marketing, but rarely more.

I was still frustrated and anxious. There had to be a better way to market myself and get new cases and clients without break-ing the bank. I also was looking for a way to get a continual flow of clients without having to pay referring attorneys a referral fee. Don't get me wrong. Attorney referrals are a great way to build a practice. However, in New York the attorney's fee on a medical malpractice case is a sliding scale that only starts at 30 percent and decreases by 5 percent as we get more and more money for the client. To give a referring attorney a large fee on top of the small fee we might generate simply didn't make good economic sense.

At that time I started to learn about websites and blogs. If you remember, in the "early days" attorneys only had static websites that contained their credentials—nothing more than what was in their Martindale-Hubbell listing. A little while later, a tiny little website came on the scene that allowed people to upload their video clips for anyone to see. I couldn't understand the point of putting video online for others to see. It just made no sense.

Want to know the name of that small video website? YouTube.

Just like attorneys had no idea what to do with their novel websites and blogs, attorneys had no idea how to use YouTube to our advantage.

Some enterprising lawyers took their TV commercials and put them on YouTube, "hoping" someone would watch their 30 seconds of drivel that said, "Come to me because I'm a lawyer and I'm here." What bothered me was that none of those TV ads ever explained why. "Why should I come to you?" "Why are you different than those other lawyers?" They never took the time to explain. I thought there had to be a better way.

NO ONE TO MENTOR ME ABOUT MARKETING

Remember, I'm still practicing law; trying cases, handling depositions, seeing new clients, and dealing with the paperwork back in the office. I'm answering the phone anytime a potential new client would call. In fact, I'd drop what I was doing to answer a new call any time of day. I had no idea that there was a better way to practice law. Nobody in law school ever explained to me the business of law.

None of the law firms I worked for ever took me aside to teach me the economics of practicing law. The bar associations didn't have classes, seminars, or experienced attorneys who would take me under their wing and explain the realities of running a real law firm. Instead, I learned by trial and error and by bouncing ideas off my close colleagues and friends. If only I knew then what I know now.

I learned pretty quickly that lawyers had no idea how to use video. Sure there were some innovative lawyers who were using their websites to educate their consumers, but those were few and far between. Most people still didn't use Google to search for things as they do now. Google was then a noun and not a verb yet.

When YouTube came online, I started to experiment with video. I didn't know any lawyer who was using it as an educational tool to educate their online viewers. There were no video companies who were teaching lawyers how to do it either. I did see some lawyers take their videotaped CLE lectures and put them online. Why? Just to put something online to show if anyone looked. The problem was that nobody was looking, and nobody wanted to watch an attorney talk for an hour about some arcane area of law.

THAT "AHA" MOMENT

It was around that time that two really smart business marketing guys started talking about education-based marketing. Having never been exposed to marketing, I was fascinated. These two people were actually advocating giving information away online. Lots of it. Information that your ideal client, consumer, or customer needed and wanted. They wrote articles and blog posts about it. They taught it. I read it. It really made sense.

By this time websites were evolving from primitive to slightly improved. Photos of lawyers started appearing on their sites.

Flash animation took over those boring lawyerly images of courthouses, gavels, and flags. Still, most lawyers didn't have a clue about education-based marketing, the premise behind which was to educate your consumer. By doing that, you established yourself as an expert without ever having to say you're an expert.

Remember when I told you that lawyers had no idea what to do with video? Well... I had an idea. I thought, why can't I create video that is educational and informative to people who are searching for a medical malpractice and personal injury attorney? Why can't I give them information in a way that *shows* them I know what I'm doing?

I was still looking for ways to effectively and ethically advertise my legal services. Paying $25,000 for a full-page ad each year was losing its novelty. Being on page 9 didn't help either. The classified ads got me zero cases. The TV ad generated a few leads, but no valid cases. The display ad generated tire kickers but no good cases. I was still doing something wrong. My referral base was good, but those lawyers also were not seeing many good medical malpractice cases.

Does Video Marketing Work?

THEY MISSED THE TUMOR RIGHT IN FRONT OF THEIR EYES

A 30-year-old home health aide was taking a patient to the doctor's office for a follow-up visit. The van she was riding in was involved in an accident, causing her to hit her head. Ironically, the accident happened right in front of the emergency room.

The hospital did everything right. They did all the right tests. They even performed an MRI of her head. "Everything was fine," they said. They sent her home to follow up with a doctor if needed. Six months later her vision got blurry. It continued to worsen day by day.

Within two months she was blind in that eye. It turns out that the MRI of her head in the emergency room showed a brain tumor that was encroaching on her optic nerve. The radiologist at the hospital actually saw this. The only problem was that nobody told the patient about it.

SCAN WITH YOUR **SMART PHONE**

This woman came to me after watching a video I created about a gentleman I represented who had lost vision in one eye. This woman's case generated a settlement of $1 million immediately prior to trial.

WORKING WITH GERRY HAS BEEN VERY REWARDING, VERY EDUCATIONAL & VERY INSPIRING

"Hello. I'm Brent Adams, a North Carolina personal injury lawyer with offices in Raleigh, Fayetteville, and Dunn, North Carolina. I just finished an amazing day with Gerry Oginski and Harry, his production assistant. And I wanted to tell you, they made me work. They made me work hard, but at the end of the day, I'm extremely happy with the product that they have produced. They have put me at ease in making videos.

They have shown me how to communicate with my potential clients and it's been an amazing process. It's been very rewarding, very educational, very inspiring. And after having received the benefit of their help and guidance, I feel that I am now prepared to prepare videos on my own – with their help, of course, and continued guidance.

But I can have the freedom and the ability to sit in my office and an idea come to me and I'll have the video camera right there, set up the video camera in just in instant, and make a video that will be projected out to my potential clients and my existing clients. And it's just been an amazing asset that I now have.

I now have the quill in my arsenal to make me a better lawyer, a more productive lawyer, a more profitable lawyer, and to help us generate some really worthwhile cases that I'm looking for. And I appreciate Gerry's and Harry's help and I would highly recommend their services to you and urge you to give them a call – sooner rather than later."

Brent Adams, Esq.
Personal Injury Attorney
119 South Lucknow Square
Dunn, NC 28334
Phone: 910.892.8177
Toll Free: 800-849-5931

SCAN WITH YOUR SMARTPHONE TO WATCH & LISTEN TO BRENT ADAMS' VIDEO.

A Budding Video Producer

I started creating video using my built-in camera on my Mac computer. I didn't have a video camera or wireless microphone or special lights. I had to ask my kids to show me how to use the iSight camera (that little pinhole webcam on my Mac) to create a video. I can laugh about it now, but when I saw the results of my first video, it was the worst thing I had ever seen. Really. It was bad.

It was dark and pixelated, and the sound was terrible. I thought that nobody would watch this because the quality was so bad. I didn't know any better, and I didn't have any video equipment that would get me better quality. What I did know was that I had content that prospective clients needed to know. I had information they needed. I knew the law. I knew how things worked. I knew how to get injured victims compensation. They didn't.

That very first video I created was like no other video online at the time. Yes, it was awful quality, but it had something that nobody else had. Useful content. The title? "How to Hire a New York Medical Malpractice Attorney." I struggled to figure out how to edit it and upload it to YouTube and was so exasperated when I watched it for the very first time online. It was even worse than it looked on my computer—more pixelated, darker, and garbled. Argghhh! Very frustrating.

I'd spend hours playing around with the video settings on my computer and the editing program to see if I could figure out, by trial and error, what the heck I did wrong. I knew I couldn't leave that video online in the condition it was in. I quickly deleted it and started over again.

I had depositions the next day and I had to prepare. I had trials coming up and had to prep my cases. I had new client meetings I had to prepare for and didn't have time to figure out how to get new clients in the door in a systematic way. I was still frustrated and angry with myself for not knowing someone who could do my marketing for me. Since my cash flow was hurting, I couldn't afford to hire a public relations company or an ad agency to handle my marketing. Social media hadn't been invented yet, and I still didn't know what to do that would turn my law firm into a self-sustaining business with a constant flow of qualified callers and clients.

I still had this nagging feeling in the back of my mind that video was the key. Video would be "it," I thought. It would allow someone looking for me to get to know me before they ever called me for an appointment.

I started looking for video production companies to teach me what I didn't know. There were no production companies willing to teach. A few independent video guys had technical tutorials explaining how video is processed and rendered. I bought a tutorial CD from a guy in New York who took three and a half hours to explain the settings he used for a video editing program I didn't have and couldn't afford. That was a waste of money and three and a half hours of my time that I'll never see again. That CD sits proudly on the shelf above my computer as a reminder of the tremendous effort and energy I put into learning how to create online video.

A REVELATION

After I redid my initial video and uploaded it, something fascinating happened. I got emails and phone calls from people who watched my video. I was amazed. "Why did you call after watching my video?" I asked. "Because you offered information that nobody else did," came the reply. (I don't give legal advice in my videos.) That got me energized and excited. I started to create videos about different topics. I edited those and uploaded them as well. It was extremely time intensive, especially since I had to do this by trial and error. YouTube was still in its infancy, and lawyers still hadn't caught on to how useful video was.

Fast forward to today. I now have over 600 educational videos that are online working for me night and day to market my solo law firm. How is it that a little solo practitioner from a suburb 20 miles outside of New York City is able to compete with the biggest law firms in Manhattan spending millions of dollars to market their law firms?

How is it that a little solo attorney is able to generate consistent calls and emails to his office?

The answer is using video.

That's my story. I'd love to hear yours.

TRADITIONAL WAY TO CLOSE A POTENTIAL CLIENT

In order to get a potential client to sign a retainer agreement during your initial consultation, you would need to dazzle them, entertain them, educate them, teach them, and otherwise be brilliant to have them realize that you are the best lawyer on the planet and could solve their every problem.

That's old school. It still works, but you've got to work so darned hard to make that happen and do it every single time a new client walks into your office. Extremely inefficient. There is a better way. A much better way.

What if you could indoctrinate your potential clients with your legal brilliance before you ever meet them or speak to them? What if you could dazzle them with your courtroom style and sharp tongue? What if you could get your new clients to beg for an appointment with you? How cool would it be if your new clients walk into your office and tell you how great you are and thank you for being such a wonderful lawyer, the moment they meet you?

Guess what? All this can and should happen. But it will only happen if you create video where your online viewers get to see you, hear you, and learn from you. The only way this can happen is if you create compelling content that your viewers want. If you give them garbage, they will resent it and not look upon you and your firm with the respect and the gravitas you deserve.

When new clients meet me for the very first time, the reaction is always the same and it never stops amazing me:

- "Mr. Oginski, thank you so much for all the wonderful content and information you provided in your videos. Nobody else provides this." (I don't give legal advice in my videos.)

- "I feel like I already know you."

- "You're exactly like you are in your videos." (I hope so!)

- "I can't believe I'm meeting you. You're like a celebrity online."

- "I feel like I've been here before."

These people have gotten to know me, like me, and trust me.

How? From my videos.

Why is that important?

Go back to the traditional way of closing the deal. Lawyer razzles and dazzles client in office for an hour. Get's exhausted. Next new client, must do same thing. Next… same razzle-dazzle. By the end of the day, you don't want to talk anymore. It's really tiring to do that over and over each day.

With video, you have presold yourself. These new clients understand I have information they want. They've watched my videos. Not just one or two or five. They watch a lot of my videos. They have come to trust what I have to say. They believe me. When they come into my office, I don't have to put on a song and dance. Instead, I just have to listen and see if we're a good fit. In cases where I reject a client, they often get upset that I will not take their case. People have literally begged me to take their cases. "I'm telling you I have a million-dollar case. I want you to take it. I don't trust other lawyers. You, I trust."

OLD SCHOOL V. NEW SCHOOL.

Which one do you prefer? Personally, after being in practice for more than 23 years and having done the old-school method for most of my career, I am more than happy to go new school and let my videos talk for me. Video works, and I'm living proof of that.

Does Video Marketing Work?

DOCTOR CAUSED PERFORATION AND FAILED TO RECOGNIZE IT

I received a phone call from a man whose mom had recently died following a routine colonoscopy procedure. The medical examiner said something about his mom dying from sepsis. The son went online to learn what sepsis is. He found a video I created titled "What is Sepsis?"

That video prompted him to call to ask for more information. That call resulted in a valid medical malpractice case that generated a settlement of $395,000.

SCAN WITH YOUR **SMART PHONE**

MY EXPECTATION WAS THAT I WOULD STAND IN FRONT OF A CAMERA, INTRODUCE MYSELF FIRST, TALK ABOUT HOW GREAT WE WERE, HOW GREAT I WAS, WHAT I CAN DO FOR THEM...BUT AFTER OUR CALL WITH GERRY...

Daniel Burke
Parker Waichman, LLP, A National Law Firm

Following our call today, I spent some time thinking about what we needed to tell our clients — prospective clients — about what we do and how we can help them. Identifying first what drug or product they happen to be using, then identifying the likely and linkable injuries with respect to that product or event.

And before our call the other day, my expectation was that I would stand in front of a camera, introduce myself first, talk about how great we were, how great I was, what I can do for them and basically how wonderful we are and why this client should come to our firm. After our call, the better way to do this and the more effective way to do this is to provide information to the clients and talk to them about what they're going through, identify for them how we're going to go about helping them (conduct an investigation on their behalf, look into their problems, and see if we can link the problems that they're having to the drug or device that they're having trouble with).

And the way of delivering this as an informational fashion as opposed to me telling the prospective clients how wonderful we are, I think this is a more effective way to communicate to the clients.

Dan Burke, Esq.
Parker Waichman
A National Law Firm
6 Harbor Park Drive
Port Washington, NY 11050
Phone: 516.466.6500

CHAPTER 2

SCAN WITH YOUR
SMARTPHONE TO
WATCH & LISTEN TO
DAN BURKE'S VIDEO.

The Worst Marketing Advice I Ever Received: "Get Your Name Out There"

You are reading this because you want to learn how to use video to market your law firm. Maybe you're a solo practitioner. Maybe you work in a small law firm having one to five attorneys. Maybe you are a senior partner in a midsize or large law firm. You are interested in taking your marketing to the next level and want to learn more.

I feel really privileged to be able to help lawyers across the country with their video marketing. Why? The answer is simple.

I'm just like you.

Six years ago when I was learning how to do this video stuff, there was nobody in the country who was teaching lawyers how to create video. If you wanted to create video, you had to find some video company to do this and it was extremely expensive. TV production companies creating TV ads were the dominant force at the time.

The problems I had then are the same ones you have now. I was in the same position you are in now. You see, I had good cases that were resolving. The problem was that I wasn't replenishing my cases fast enough. The traditional forms of lawyer marketing that I had used in the past were not generating the types of calls or cases that I wanted. That was extremely frustrating.

What was I doing that prevented me from getting cases that my competitors were getting? I didn't know the answer, so I started looking for it. I started to read about marketing. I started buying marketing "systems" that would supposedly turn my law practice into a case-generating machine. Hah! I was so green.

There was one marketing product that was highly advertised in my local bar association journal. It sounded perfect. I spent $2,500 thinking this was the answer. What a joke. It was run by a guy who's not even an attorney.

The point of this program was to create time-urgency reports and send people nasty and obnoxious follow-up cards and letters telling them that if they did not respond by a certain date, stamped in red, they would lose the opportunity to work with me.

I devoured the material in a weekend and then followed the instructions to the letter. By the time I started implementing this magic bullet system, I came to the conclusion that this was the stupidest thing I had done.

I wanted my money back, but felt guilty since I read all the material and found it was useless.

THERE HAD TO BE A BETTER WAY

I kept looking for more and diverse ways to generate calls to my office.

Yellow Pages

I spent $25,000 on a full-page ad each year on page 9 in the most competitive market in New York. The problem with being on page 9 is that consumers start at page 1 of the lawyer's section. The only reason they would call me is because eight other lawyers ahead of me rejected their case. After a while, I would start every phone call with "Tell me why the eight lawyers you called before me rejected your case."

TV Advertising

I tried TV advertising. I created the same crappy 30-second commercial that every lawyer in the world created.

"Have you been injured? [siren in the background]

Hurt in a car accident? [picture of gruesome car crash]

If so, you need to call me. [close-up shot of me]

I can help.

We have free parking [image of parking lot]

and years of experience. [picture of diplomas] Call the law firm of Gerald Oginski…"

That was frustrating.

I didn't know how to be different. I didn't know how to advertise or market myself. I was just copying every lawyer who copied every other lawyer.

Newspaper Advertising

I did newspaper display advertising. But I didn't know how to write copy. I didn't even know what "copy" was. I was just copying the other lawyer ads I had seen in newspapers and magazines. Basically it listed every type of case I ever handled.

- Car accidents

- Trip and fall

- Slip and fall

- Wrongful death

- Medical malpractice

- Product liability

- Premises liability

- Bus accidents

- Truck crashes

- Bicycle Injuries

- Construction accidents

- Podiatry errors

- Dog bites

- Dentist errors

- Medical errors

It was the same useless ad that failed to identify my ideal client and ideal case. At that time I didn't even know who my ideal client was. "Free parking," "15 years of experience," blah, blah, blah. Every lawyer said the same exact thing. I did have enough sense to put my picture in my ad. Big whoop. I didn't know it at the time, but nobody cared what I looked like. I often wondered if I would have generated more calls if I put on a clown costume.

Classified Ads

I even dug down into the depths of classified ads thinking it would be different, in that it might generate something. I was wrong. All the lawyers who advertised in the classifieds were doing the same exact type of marketing.

I thought, incorrectly, that by putting an eight-word ad in the classifieds, that would somehow be enough to generate calls to my office. Was I green. I figured that since other lawyers were using classifieds, they must be getting calls that were paying for the ads.

I honestly had no clue and nobody to turn to for answers. It wasn't like you could pick up the phone and call your competitor to ask him whether his classified ads were generating calls and income because you wanted to do the same thing.

"Hey John, listen… you don't know me and I'm a personal injury lawyer just like you. I see your classified ads all the time in the New York Post… are they working for you?" "Yeah, the reason I ask is that I want to do the same thing, and if they're doing well for you, then I think I'm going to try it too…"

Yeah. Good luck asking your competitor that question.

EVERYBODY ELSE IS DOING IT

The yellow pages marketing rep kept telling me to "get my name out there" by continuing to put out ads explaining the different areas of law that I practice.

I was getting desperate. I was copying what everybody else was doing, believing that if they were spending money to invest in these different types of advertising media, they must be doing something right, otherwise they would not be investing in these efforts.

That was the deadly mistake I made. I assumed that because all these lawyers were spending money on different forms of "getting their name out there" and doing it the same way that everybody else was doing, that automatically meant they were generating results.

The reality is that there was a big disconnect. I never picked up the phone to call any of these lawyers to ask them what type of results or successes or failures they were having from these marketing methods. I felt they would never share that information with me, so why should I even make the effort to call?

THE PURPOSE OF LEGAL MARKETING

I'm sure when you went to law school you did so with every intention of being the best lawyer you could be. Many of you went to work for a law firm with the intention of learning.

You got paid to practice law. You were helping people solve their legal problems. You may have had mentors or experienced lawyers you could turn to for advice. However, most of you have never been taught how to get new cases. Most lawyers coming out of law school have no idea how to make it rain.

There are no law professors in law school who teach you about the economics of practicing law. Nobody teaches you what you need to do to develop a list of clients who want you. No one explains how to set up a referral network. Rather, the law schools focus on the substantive law and hope that you'll learn as you go.

Seems to me that's a pretty pathetic way to teach lawyers and then throw them into the marketplace and let them fend for themselves. I am not going to address the motives for why law schools don't teach marketing. Nor will I address why most bar associations don't actively teach it either. Just as our law schools shun legal marketing, so do many bar associations.

Unless you're born with a silver spoon in your mouth and go to work for a family law firm, or you find a trusted mentor who teaches you the practice of law from the inside out, you're like many of us who simply have no clue.

Some lawyers scramble to learn this out of necessity. They may have been fired, let go, or downsized from their position. Others may have chosen to strike out on their own. Either way, the need to understand legal marketing is key to a successful legal career.

Since there are no "official" legal marketing law school classes or regular bar association lectures about marketing, an entire cottage industry has developed to help lawyers learn and understand the business of law.

You may also have heard the saying "If I only knew then, what I know now," which typically refers to some idea or money-making strategy that would have dramatically improved your business had you know it earlier in time. That saying is appropriate for me and many lawyers I know.

There are many ways to successfully market your law firm. The smart lawyers learn all they can from smarter attorneys who have already done it and are doing it well. Referrals, newsletters, websites, social networks, TV, radio, display ads, 1-800 numbers, charity involvement, and networking events all help.

The reality is that there is no one single thing or silver bullet that will make you successful as a lawyer. Being a great lawyer is only one key component to success. Learning how to market your law firm is the next key.

Suggestion: Become a student of marketing. Go to legal marketing seminars that some of the bigger, well-known attorneys put on. Learn as much as you can to see what works and what doesn't. Don't copy someone else's marketing unless you know exactly what their return on investment is. Copying an attorney's yellow pages ad, TV spot, or educational video will not help you understand what goes on behind the scenes.

Become a legal marketing student and you'll understand the practice of law through entirely different eyes. Guaranteed.

Does Video Marketing Work?

DAD FALLS FROM HOSPITAL BED AND DIES THREE WEEKS LATER

I received a call from Annie. She was frantic. Her dad had recently been diagnosed with lung cancer and was in the hospital being treated. Because he was agitated, he was physically restrained to the bed so he would not fall and hurt himself.

Annie received a call from the hospital one night letting her know that her dad had fallen out of bed, hit his head, and was now in a coma. He died three weeks later from blunt-force trauma to the head.

Annie went online to search for information about falls from hospital beds and found my videos discussing that exact topic. Her call turned into a valid case. I settled that case for $300,000 during mediation after finishing defendants' depositions.

SCAN WITH YOUR **SMART PHONE**

THEY WERE NOT WHAT I WAS LOOKING FOR, EXCEPT FOR GERRY OGINSKI. HE IS A LAWYER. HE UNDERSTOOD SPECIFICALLY WHAT MY NEEDS WERE... GERRY WAS THE ONE WHO STOOD COMPLETELY HEAD AND SHOULDERS ABOVE ANYBODY ELSE OUT THERE.

"I'm Jeff Helsdon and I'm a real estate and business lawyer in Fircrest, Washington.

Well, for some time, my partner and I realized that the future for marketing our law practice is going to be the creation of video so that people who are looking for lawyers can go out there and see and hear and develop a relationship with the lawyer and that's the first impression that we're going to be able to give to people.

I actually looked at trying to do this on my own and was going to attempt to do that first. Having done the research on all of the component parts that it would take for me to put a very professional-looking and sounding video together that was educational in nature was such a daunting task. I realized that the amount of time that I would take in putting that together did not warrant my going through that process if there was a better alternative.

I went on the internet and I looked up what kind of production companies are out there producing the kind of videos that I was interested in, which are videos by lawyers for the public; the public asking questions about specific items of interest to them in their effort to find a lawyer. And really, I was dissatisfied with the vast majority of the videos that were out there.

They were not what I was looking for, except for Gerry Oginski. He is a lawyer. He understood specifically what my needs were because he has a small firm practice. We have a small firm practice; it's a boutique practice and we were looking for someone who understood our needs and had the expertise to be able to pull all of the necessary components of producing a video and getting it uploaded that we needed and Gerry was the one who stood completely head and shoulders above anybody else out there.

Well as I speak to you, it's about quarter after 4 in the afternoon and we've been shooting video since about 8 o'clock this morning and doing it non-stop even through lunch and I have to say that my expectations this morning were a little uncertain.

I didn't know if I was going to have difficulties in projecting myself and presenting the points that I wanted to make, but Gerry was able to work myself and my partner and my associate through this process so that it became almost flawless and seamless. If you make a mistake as you're producing the video, he works you through it. By the end of the day, each of us was producing video and speaking on camera in such a way that seems like we've been doing this as second nature for a long period of time. He really works through this very well for us."

Jeff Helsdon, Esq.
Real Estate & Business Attorney
Oldfield & Helsdon
1401 Regents Blvd., Suite 102
Fircrest, Washington 98466
253-564-9500

SCAN WITH YOUR SMARTPHONE TO WATCH & LISTEN TO JEFF HELSDON'S VIDEO.

How Are You Different?

One day a really good friend of mine asked me a question. He said that if all lawyers are advertising in the yellow pages, how does a consumer know that you are different or special and are the right one for them?

That got me thinking. How do we as attorneys distinguish ourselves?

Does an offer of free parking set you apart? The fact that I am caring, does that help a consumer decide to come to me instead of my competitor?

What do I do that would get a consumer to come to me instead of my colleague? I was having a difficult time answering that question.

If I could not answer that question in my own mind and help a consumer recognize the distinction, then a consumer looking for an attorney would not be able to tell the difference either.

WAITING FOR THE PHONE TO RING

It's 2006. Here I am sitting in my office waiting for the phone to ring, hoping that the next case will be a good one to get me over the hump. My secretary asked me every day what I was doing to generate more cases. She even came right out and said that if I don't get more cases soon, there's no way for me to pay my bills or her salary.

I was getting desperate to find different ways to generate new calls to the office.

I had always thought that my reputation and my prior experience would be enough to generate referrals to me. They did. Just not enough. I had a good referral network, but in my niche—handling primarily medical malpractice—out of 100 calls I immediately reject 99 of them. That's just on the phone! Of the people I invite into my office, I reject two-thirds of them after doing a full-blown investigation.

Unlike a car accident attorney who can take pretty much everything that walks in the door, handling medical malpractice cases in New York is very different. You must be highly selective. Each case lasts an average of two to three years. Each case I take on is a very significant financial commitment.

Waiting for the phone to ring just doesn't cut it in your law practice. If you wait around you lose cases. Your competitors will snatch up those cases you could have had. That leaves you staring at the phone wondering what to do next.

HOW DID I KNOW THAT VIDEO WOULD WORK?

In the beginning of the online video era, I was starting to learn about something called education-based marketing. There were two really smart guys that I was starting to follow. One was a businessman named David Frey, who was helping pool and spa owners market themselves. The other was a legal marketing guy named Trey Ryder. Both of these guys believed that by educating your consumers you'd be able to attract them. This was a fascinating concept.

At the same time, I knew there had to be a better way to try and educate my consumers beyond the traditional forms of media that were already being used. Being a technology junkie and having a Mac computer, I wondered whether there was any way to create video to put something online to educate my consumers.

It was exactly at that time that YouTube had just started up. Nobody had any idea what to do with that website. It said it was accepting "user-generated content." When I first saw that, I didn't think there was any way that I as a lawyer could possibly use it to my benefit. I thought initially that nobody would waste their time creating video that other people would want to watch.

I remember exploring their new website and I saw one or two lawyer ads or commercials that had been posted. I could not understand why a video company would put a TV ad for a lawyer on this video site.

CHAPTER 4

Nobody wanted to watch a lawyer commercial, since the lawyer never took the time to explain why anybody should come to them. A typical TV ad was 30 seconds long and screamed at you, telling you to pick up the phone and call now. There was no way to distinguish one lawyer from another with these TV ads.

THE PROBLEM WITH TV ADS

Let's get back to the TV ads that lawyers traditionally used to attract new cases. Every time you wanted to get more cases, you would have to run more TV ad campaigns. Then of course you needed an entire staff to handle the inbound calls, especially if your ads were running after normal business hours.

When I talk to lawyers today who use TV advertising as their main means of marketing, most have a difficult time transitioning to video marketing online. The reason is because video marketing requires an entirely different mindset than TV-based, interruption-style marketing. Although the purpose of marketing is the same, i.e., to get somebody to call after seeing your message, people respond to TV ads differently than to videos on a website.

WHY VIDEO IS DIFFERENT

With online video, your consumers are actively looking for information from you.

In a TV ad, nobody is looking for your ad. It just happens to catch you at that moment and interrupt your TV show you were watching. If your ad is compelling enough, then you may be prompted to catch the 800 number and call immediately. If you neglect to write down the number, I can pretty much guarantee that within 15 minutes you will see another ad for a different lawyer with a different 800 number. Chances are you may grab a pen at that point and call that lawyer and forget about the original one who interrupted your viewing pleasure.

Unlike interruption-based marketing, when a consumer goes online to look for information about their particular medical or legal problem, they want to learn. They don't want to be pitched to, nor do they want to be sold to. They are in search mode and are looking for information to help them make a decision about what to do next. You have to give them information they need to know, otherwise they will go elsewhere.

VIDEO ALLOWS YOU TO COMMUNICATE

TV ads do not allow you to communicate. Instead they scream at you and demand that you do something immediately. They often start out with the question and end with the direction to take immediate action by calling now. That is known as direct-response marketing.

In contrast, people who go online to search for information want to learn as much as possible about their legal problem. They want to learn about their medical problem. They want to learn about other people in similar situations. They want to learn how cases like theirs have been resolved. They want to learn about the lawyers who represent people with similar cases.

A television ad that is thrown online or on your website is an extremely poor way to convert a viewer into a caller. Remember, those TV ads do nothing to educate a viewer. The viewer learns nothing about a particular case that you may have handled, what you did to help them, or the ultimate outcome you were able to achieve.

You want your viewer to automatically assume that you have experience simply because you say you do. If you really do have that experience, then prove it. Show your viewer *action*. Show them you have been in the trenches and what it means for them and their particular problem. It is never good enough to say that you have been in practice for 20 years.

"We've been in practice for a combined total of 57 years."

So what?

The length of time you are in practice may not always be a benefit. There are many younger attorneys who are better than you at trial, in court, and on papers. They may be better communicators. They may be able to better explain them-selves to their clients and consumers.

However, all is not lost. You still have the ability to set yourself apart from all of your competitors. The way to do that is with video.

WHAT'S SO COMPELLING AND DIFFERENT ABOUT YOU?

I ask lawyers that question all the time now. It typically stops them dead in their tracks. They stop in midsentence, look up toward the sky, and think about the answer to that question. Most lawyers have never asked themselves that question. If they had, they would have come up with some answers. Here are their typical responses:

- "I care."

- "I give personal attention."

- "I make sure to return all phone calls within 24 hours."

- "I return all emails within two hours."

- "My door is always open."

- "I graduated from the best law school and won all these awards."

- "I published all these great articles and chapters in textbooks."

- "I lecture to the bar associations all the time."

Remember when you were in second grade and your mother told you that you were "special"? It's true. You are. You're unique. You're different than everybody else.

The problem is that we, as attorneys, all do the same thing. We all know the law. Some better than others. Some more experienced than others. If we all know the same law, why is it that some lawyers are able to attract really good cases, while others continually struggle to do so?

The answer is marketing.

We are all trying to market our services as lawyers. It doesn't matter what our specialty is or what our niche is. The bottom line is that if you cannot differentiate yourself, your viewer will be unable to do so either.

Therefore it is necessary for you to stand out from the crowd and to show that you are different. That difference may be minor, but may be enough to show your viewer that you are the one they want.

Maybe you sound better. Maybe you look better. Maybe you are more confident. Whatever it is that makes you special is what you should focus on in your marketing.

Really smart attorneys attract people because of their personalities and their marketing. Think about it. We, as attorneys, know the law. Our clients and consumers do not. Our clients have legal problems. We have solutions. Most of the solutions are not novel or groundbreaking. If true, why is it that the successful lawyers continue to bring in the winners, while others can't find clients?

Again, the answer has to do with how the public sees and perceives you. Can they find you? Do they know you exist? How do you reach out to them? What do you do to educate and teach your potential clients?

By taking the time to explain, you show you're different. By reaching out and helping someone understand what to expect, you show you're different than your competitors.

By being different (and totally within your ethical rules) you will stand out from the rest and get noticed.

How best can you do that? You know the answer.

In case you didn't … it's using video.

Ask yourself how a solo attorney in a suburb 20 miles outside of Manhattan is able to compete in the most competitive market in the country against bigger law firms with more resources. Ask yourself how one solo attorney is able to consistently get his website to come up in the number one organic search-result position on Google, beating out lots of other law firms without paying a single dime to anyone to make that happen.

Ask yourself how a little solo attorney is able to generate 8–10 calls per day. Ask yourself how one person with a staff of one paralegal is able to practice law and help lawyers across the country market their practices online using the best media available.

The answer is... with video.

Video has allowed me the opportunity to show that I am different. It has given me the opportunity to explain to my potential clients information they need to know. It has given me the chance to be creative in an online frontier that has no rules or boundaries other than the ethical rules that we attorneys are all bound by.

If you cannot answer the question "What is different about you?" then you will never be able to market yourself effectively.

Does Video Marketing Work?

WOMAN HAS BUNION SURGERY, DIES NINE MONTHS LATER

I received a call one day from a gentleman down south whose mom had recently died. He didn't understand why she died but did know that she had foot surgery nine months earlier. He went online to learn about podiatry malpractice in New York. He called me after watching a video I created about podiatry injuries.

It turns out that his mom had bunion surgery. The surgery was done properly. The problem was that the foot doctor failed to recognize a postoperative infection. That infection went deep down into the bone. That's known as osteomyelitis. The failure to diagnose her osteomyelitis ultimately caused her death. My medical experts concluded that had the podiatrist timely recognized her infection and treated her, she would be alive today. I settled that case for $495,000.

SCAN WITH YOUR **SMARTPHONE**

ANYBODY WHO'S CONSIDERING GERRY OGINSKI FOR VIDEO MARKETING, THERE SHOULD BE NO ONE ELSE THAT YOU SHOULD CONSIDER.

Andrew Siegel
Siegel & Coonerty, LLP, Attorneys at Law

"The reason why I chose you Gerry is very simple. You're an experienced lawyer, you're a tenured lawyer. You understand the process of being a lawyer. And now here you are, doing lawyer video. I can't imagine a more credible background for someone to video lawyers than a lawyer himself. The reason I hired you is because I've known you this long and I've never known you not to achieve something that you've put your mind to.

Spending the day with you here is just another example of Gerry Oginski achieving. You prepared us well, you required us to submit things. You literally made us do our homework in our own best interest that I can say was one of the keys to today's success. During the videotaping, you would stop and correct us when we needed correcting. During the videotaping, you let us go along on topics that you felt were interesting that may not be direct to the point but would capture our audience. When we were shy a topic, you threw one out at us. When we needed to be given direction, you gave us that direction.

I can only say to anybody who's considering Gerry Oginski for this process, that there should be no one else that you should consider."

Andrew Siegel, Esq.
NY Personal Injury Trial Lawyer
Siegel & Coonerty, LLP
419 Park Avenue South
7th Floor
New York, NY 10016
212-532-0532

SCAN WITH YOUR SMARTPHONE TO WATCH & LISTEN TO ANDREW SIEGEL'S VIDEO.

A Revolutionary Idea

Six years ago I had an idea. Why couldn't I use video to create an educational piece of information to put online? I thought that if education-based marketing worked in written form, I believed it would work even better in video form. That was the idea. The problem was executing it.

MY COMPUTER SHOOTS VIDEO

Anyone with an iMac computer had a tiny webcam built into it. The only problem was that I had no idea how to use it and had to ask my kids how to turn the camera on. It could take really cool pictures using iPhoto, but I had no idea how to create a video file and what to do with it afterwards.

My kids finally showed me how to press the record button and start talking. I figured I would learn as I went. So here is what I did.

I'm sitting in my second-floor office at home. I did not want viewers to see where I was creating the video so I put up a screen behind me. I knew nothing about lighting or audio, and I figured I might as well use whatever I had and that would be fine.

In order to get good audio, I had to sit pretty close to the computer. That meant that I had to sit about 6–7 inches away from the computer monitor. It also meant that the reflection of the monitor would be visible in my eyeglasses.

Since I would be reading part of what I wanted to talk about, the information would be on the computer screen.

MY SCREEN DEBUT

I dressed up for the video. I put on a shirt, tie, and jacket, but decided since I was doing this at home and the camera wouldn't see me below my waist, it would be okay for me to wear shorts. I wonder if TV news anchors do the same thing.

The very first video I created was titled "How to Hire a Medical Malpractice Lawyer in New York." It was the worst video I ever created. The lighting was horrible. The video was pixelated. The background was dull and uninspiring. The reflection in my eyeglasses was clearly evident. From a quality production standpoint, this video was downright awful. The good thing was that I didn't know any better.

I posted this video on YouTube. I had no idea what to expect. All I knew was that there was nobody in the country who was creating an educational video message to market their law practice online. I didn't know it at the time, but I was a pioneer with this type of video marketing.

Despite this video being awful, it generated calls to my office. I was shocked the first few times I received calls from people who saw my video and wanted more information.

I was excited. I was fascinated.

I asked these people lots of questions about how they found my video and what they found interesting about it. I still have that video online today. If you search the title "How to Hire a Medical Malpractice Lawyer in New York" you will find it. You should watch it. You will laugh. Don't laugh too hard since the calls I received from that video generated valid cases and fees.

That was the beginning of the video marketing revolution for lawyers.

BLOGS ARE ALL THE RAGE

Fast forward to the present. Facebook has taken over the Internet. Google and YouTube run a distant second and third place. Online content is 60–70 percent video and growing each day. Forty-eight hours of video are uploaded to YouTube every minute. Billions of videos are watched monthly. You know why, don't you? People are lazy. They don't want to read.

People go online for two primary reasons: (1) to be entertained, or (2) for information. If they have an option of being spoon-fed information via a video, where they don't have to do any heavy lifting or reading, the majority will choose video.

Most older lawyers are technophobes. Not the younger generation though. Still, many midsize and large law firms are reluctant to put their attorneys on video for two reasons:

(1) They do their marketing by committee and nobody can ever make a decision, and

(2) They don't know what to do with video and how to effectively leverage their knowledge and expertise with their message. Solos and small law firms have a distinct advantage over their larger counterparts. We can make decisions on the fly. We can decide to take imperfect action. Smart lawyers recognize that even imperfect action is better than no action.

Does Video Marketing Work?

A UROLOGY NIGHTMARE RESULTS IN SETTLEMENT OF $850,000

A gentleman began to have difficulty urinating, and the doctor opened the scar tissue within his urethra. This was a temporary fix and the patient was back weeks and months later. The doctor decided to insert a stent into the man's penis. Not only did he insert one stent, but he inserted two stents. What the doctor didn't realize was that using stents in a young man was contraindicated, since they were known to cause severe pain every time he would get an erection.

The doctor then decided to remove the stents, and in doing so tore apart the man's urethra. He needed major reconstructive urological surgery that required a urinary diversion in order for him to urinate. The hole to urinate was located between his scrotum and his anus and required him to sit down every time he needed to pee.

This man came to me after searching online for information about urethral stents. He found a video I created about urology malpractice. He liked what he saw and then picked up the phone to talk to me. I settled his case for $850,000 during mediation immediately before trial.

SCAN WITH YOUR
SMARTPHONE

THERE WAS NO QUESTION IN MY MIND WHO COULD HELP ME IMPROVE AND GROW MY PRACTICE...AND THAT WAS GERRY

"Hi, I'm Jack Carney-DeBord, Ohio divorce and personal injury attorney from Delaware, Ohio. I came to Gerry Oginski for several reasons. Number one, because I wanted to improve my business. I wanted a platform to send out to Central Ohio and Ohio claimants who may have been injured by car accident, motorcycle or truck accident and who want more education. I wanted also to reach divorce clients. I have been asked the same questions over and over for 18 years and I wanted the opportunity to get those answers into video and onto my website.

When I did my research, when I looked on the Web, when I talked to other attorneys, there was one man who I thought could do the job and that was Gerry Oginski.

Gerry's been here since early this morning and we have worked minute-by-minute, video-by-video to improve each and every aspect of my performance. I can't tell you how much I've been impressed, I can't tell you how much how I have improved from morning to afternoon to now.

I thank him, I suggest and recommend him highly. If you're considering improving your business, and want to use the tool of video, this is a great place to start. I chose the Lawyers' Video Studio for a couple simple reasons.

Number one, I could find nowhere, no how, an attorney who's experienced in personal injury and litigation types of cases who is teaching, who is teaching, who is showing, who is educating other attorneys on what to do. I had no idea what to do, and I found absolutely no one who was doing this.

Number two, I had some decisions to make. There were other video people. I interviewed them. I learned that in one day with Gerry Oginski I felt that could launch videos that would help me improve and grow my practice. And when I looked at all that, there was no question in my mind who that man was and whose Lawyers Video company that was. And that was Gerry's.

The mastermind call was very essential. What I had done, though, even before the mastermind was I had looked at almost every one of Gerry's videos, so I had an idea. What this did was made me put pencil to paper in an outline form of exactly what he expected as we approached the day he would come to my office. He told me have so many videos.

For example, 5 videos on 5 of your top cases. He told me to have 5 frequently-asked questions for each area of my practice. The mastermind call was terrific. It gave me an outline, it made me put pen to paper to what I needed to do to get prepared for our big day here at my office. When Gerry walked in my office, within 5 minutes, we had started the process. We had opened the boxes; we got the equipment out and were beginning the road to do the job that they had come here to do.

I was extremely impressed with the details, with how they calmed my nerves, with how they moved through the course of the day to improve the videos, they showed me what was going on by replaying them and gave me tips that each time I did a subject area, I felt I improved.

Harry (Gerry's partner) was terrific. He arranged all the equipment, particularly the lighting. He was looking me right in the eye as we proceeded throughout the course of the day. He was absolutely terrific, encouraging me to the point where I really felt comfortable that what I was doing behind the video here or in front of the video here was really the right thing.

I intend one thing and that is to use it, to take it outside of the office, to use it as things happen in the practice, to bring people up to date through the use of the video, and attaching them to my website. I intend to use them for personal use. I intend to share them with my kids and my wife who have their own interests as we go forward. In closing, I would like to thank Gerry and thank Harry for coming here today, all the way to Delaware, Ohio, for being on time, for giving me everything that they had promised and most importantly, for making me feel comfortable and confident that I could actually perform on a video where somebody would actually come onto my video and I could end up just like Gerry does every day with an email on my Blackberry saying "I need your help."

Jack Carney DeBord, Esq.
Personal Injury & Divorce Attorney
Jack's Law Office
305 South Sandusky Street
Delaware, OH 43015
(740) 369-7567

SCAN WITH YOUR SMARTPHONE TO WATCH & LISTEN TO JACK CARNEY DEBORD'S VIDEO.

Sharing the Vision

Fast-forward again to the present. I have created over 600 videos to market my solo practice with great success. Every month I add more fresh new video content. As I became more proficient at creating video, I kept thinking to myself: how can I use this knowledge and information to help my fellow attorneys do the same exact thing? The Lawyers' Video Studio was born out of the idea that I could help other lawyers across the country do the same thing that I have done to market my law practice.

Today you have many more resources available to teach you and help you do the type of video marketing that has worked for me in my practice. You can do the same, you just need to know how.

You can go online now and learn how to create great quality video. You can learn how to optimize your video and how to use social media to tell the world about yourself. You can learn what to talk about in a new video. And if you are a do-it-yourselfer like I am, you can learn how to do all this stuff on your own.

If you don't have any interest in learning how to do this on your own, there are many video companies out there to help you create video to market your practice without you learning how to do any of the technical stuff.

It's just like anything else. You can learn how to fix your roof if you get a leak. You can learn how to fix your leaky faucet and how to fix the transmission in your car, and even how to fix your watch when it breaks down. The question you must answer is "Do you have the time, desire, and inclination to learn how to do all these things on your own? Or, would you rather have an experienced professional handle these things for you?"

You are the only one who can answer that question.

A MILLION DOLLAR STRATEGY YOU CAN COPY

Recently the newspapers reported that the best-selling breast cancer treatment drug Avastin, was pulled off the market because the FDA found that the medication produced more harm than benefit. I immediately created a video about this news report.

Why would I do that?

I do not handle product liability cases. I do not handle defective products or do any type of drug litigation. I do not handle mass torts or toxic tort cases. Why then would a solo medical malpractice and personal injury trial lawyer in New York create a video about Avastin being pulled off the market?

If you understand the concept I'm about to teach you, it will revolutionize the way you market your practice and create content for your videos.

This particular medication was used to treat advanced forms of breast cancer. Apparently it had many side effects that were causing significant harm to patients who took it. Doctors are still allowed to prescribe this medication in an "off-label" manner with the proviso that patients are made fully aware of the significant risks associated with taking this medication.

This video had nothing to do with the fact that the FDA pulled the drug off the market. Nor did it have anything to do with side effects or injuries the medication may have caused. Instead, it had to do directly with patients who were impacted by the medication. Think about the patients who were taking this medication. They are patients who were being treated for various stages of breast cancer.

What types of cases do I handle?

Failure to diagnose cases.

I can pretty much guarantee that a percentage of those patients have nagging doubts in the back of their mind about whether their breast cancer was timely diagnosed. My video "talks" to those people. It not only educates them but gives them information they need to know concerning delay in diagnosis cases.

I want you to read that paragraph again.

When I first told you that I created a video about a drug that was pulled off the market, I'm sure you wondered why I would create such a video. I'm positive that when I told you what type of law I practiced, you were scratching your head wondering why I would bother to create a video about a possibly defective product. Remember, my video had nothing to do with asking people to call me about defective products or injury suffered because of the medication that was now pulled off the market. Instead, it was laser-directed at the people who were affected by this medication.

This strategy alone is worth millions of dollars for lawyers who are able to implement it effectively in their marketing. This strategy is but one that I teach attorneys who participate in my Total Online Video Success Program about the type of content to create when shooting their videos.

Why am I different?

There is no other *video marketing company* in the country that is run by a practicing trial attorney. I have yet to find a single video marketing company that provides the same type of ideas, tips, and strategies to help you create compelling content that gets viewers interested in what you have to say.

I write hundreds of video marketing articles a year, and have helped lawyers across the country understand the type of content they need to create to stand out from the crowd and show that they are different. I also lecture to attorneys across the country at legal marketing seminars to help them understand that they can create video using the tips and tactics I teach to create effective video.

I get great enjoyment knowing that lawyers are using my strategies to market their law firms online.

Does Video Marketing Work?

BOTCHED DELIVERY CAUSES BRAIN DAMAGE

A distraught father whose baby was just diagnosed with cerebral palsy picked up the phone to call me. His wife had just given birth and he was freaking out. He went online to learn more about this condition and came across my video discussing cerebral palsy. He eagerly wanted more information.

That phone call revealed a possible case which in turn led to a full investigation of his matter. A thorough investigation revealed significant departures from good and accepted care that resulted in an untimely delivery and brain damage to his newborn son.

That phone call to my office resulted in a valid medical malpractice case in New York that generated a settlement of $5.1 million.

The cases I have mentioned provide an insight into what I have been able to accomplish with video marketing for my solo practice in the most competitive market in the country. Each of these cases can be verified along with the settlement amounts.

SCAN WITH YOUR **SMART PHONE**

I WOULD ADVISE ANY LAWYER, IF YOU'RE CONSIDERING GOING INTO VIDEO, GO TO GERRY

"When Gerry told me we were going to do 50 videos in one day, I thought OK, sure right. I had no idea that you could actually do that.

But he has got a unique style and brings a certain skill set to the whole enterprise and I don't think a normal and I shouldn't say normal, run of the mill producer would bring. Because his background as a trial attorney gives him invaluable insights as we do the videos.

Well, it was important to me. I met Gerry at a marketing seminar. And after talking to him and doing some research on him, I decided this was the guy I wanted to work with as far as developing video content on my website because he brings a unique perspective to it, to the whole operation. As a trial attorney, he can sit there and talk on a same level as I do as a trial attorney where I wouldn't have that rapport with a regular TV producer.

He can pull us back because we all tend to talk on jargon; we all tend to talk in legalese. He forces you to get it down to the level where normal people, regular people, can understand. So we found that invaluable.

Gerry's style is not just to come in town and start shooting video. Gerry spends over an hour with you on the phone, in addition to sending you clarifying questions; questions that make you focus on what the task is at hand. And we go through those questions and start clarifying exactly what we're trying to do with these videos and the best way to present them.

The mastermind call is invaluable because, you know, you're thinking how am I going to get enough content together for 50 videos? But his questions make you focus break this down into certain digestible subjects for the layperson that's going to be watching this on the internet.

I would not even consider doing my own video because I've seen some of the results of Gerry's work and it's very professional, very smooth. If I did a video, it would look like a home video. And that's not what you want to put out. You want to put out a polished, professional image to the people you're trying to get to.

Gerry has a unique approach here. It's basically a turnkey approach in that he does a lot of preparation before he ever comes to your office. He has the mastermind session with you, you sit down and clarify the issues, you talk about what you're trying to do. And he also gives you written material that helps you focus your attention on the type of material you want to present. In addition, when he comes in he brings in all the equipment.

The advantage is that after you spend a day with Gerry, you might be tired but your work is done. His is just starting. He takes your videos, he edits them down, he puts on the graphics and he presents you with a finished product where it goes right up on YouTube, on a regular basis and are released on a monthly basis. That's not even to mention technical details I wouldn't have been able to guess at, as a layperson.

Gerry has a unique skill set, not only as a trial lawyer but also in the video field. You know, when I signed up with Gerry even when going through the mastermind session, even when going through all the written material he sent me, I really wasn't quite sure what to expect on the day of the filming.

Both Gerry and his cameraman are here, right on time, and we went right to work on the material that we developed beforehand. And we scouted out different places in the office and took different shots and changed clothes and presented a polished product. I could recommend Gerry unabashedly. I would tell anybody that this is the guy to go to. Because he is a trial lawyer, he talks our language, but yet he can help you get it down to the level it needs to be to connect with the people watching the video too. He's an expert at the actual technical aspects of it, something that I don't have time to learn how to do. And someone I would pay out the nose to someone who isn't a lawyer.

So this is unique: Gerry's trial skills and also his technical skills combine to form a finished product that is well worth the money. I would advise anybody at all, if you're considering going into video, which you should consider going into video because it's going to become increasingly important in the years to come – go to Gerry."

David Glatthorn, Esq.
Personal Injury Trial Lawyer
David Glatthorn Law
506-A Datura Street
West Palm Beach, FL 33401
Phone: 561-659-1999
Toll Free: 888-340-2620

SCAN WITH YOUR SMARTPHONE TO
WATCH & LISTEN TO DAVID
GLATTHORN'S VIDEO.

How to Convert a Viewer into a Caller

There is an art and science to creating and promoting your videos. There's so much to learn about video marketing and distribution through YouTube that this could easily be an upper-level business school or postgrad class. Pressing the red record button and then directly uploading to YouTube is never your goal. There is much more to be done in order to maximize the chances that your video will be found and watched.

Your goal in creating video is to teach, educate, and inform. That is only the first goal. The primary goal in your mind should always be to create video that converts a viewer into a caller. You cannot begin to convert a viewer into a caller if all you know is traditional forms of attorney advertising. If you try and use traditional forms of TV advertising, yellow pages advertising, and the like, and simply apply that to video marketing, you will fail miserably. Guaranteed.

Let me explain why. In 2006 when YouTube first came on the scene, there were video companies and lawyers who took their 30-second TV ads and put them online, believing that viewers would want to watch their TV commercials online. But they soon learned that viewers had no interest in watching a TV commercial online. Why not?

The answer is simple. The people who were going online wanted information. That's why they were searching. Lawyer TV ads did nothing to help the viewer understand the topic and information they were searching for. Yet lawyers and their video companies continued to put their TV ads online.

Some marketing gurus convince lawyers that they should create PowerPoint presentations that are narrated and add some background music to drive traffic. Again, a lawyer who creates "video" that way fails to realize the most basic motivating psychology that explains why video is so powerful.

WHY VIDEO WORKS

The reason why video works so well is that you have the ability to teach and explain. You have the ability to talk for a few minutes and explain why. TV commercials don't do that. A narrative PowerPoint presentation doesn't do that.

Also, your goal when creating video is to connect and create a bond with your online viewer. Your viewer gets to see you. Your viewer gets to hear you. Your viewer begins to trust you. You cannot do that with a PowerPoint presentation or a slide show.

Some amazing statistics: Forty-eight hours of video are uploaded every minute to YouTube. YouTube is the second largest search engine in the world, directly behind Google.

If you think video is a fad, you'd be 100 percent wrong. Video has revolutionized the way lawyers and businesses market themselves. Never before have people been able to see, virtually touch, and hear what an attorney has to say before meeting them in person.

YouTube has given us a way to get our videos found, clicked on, and watched. Importantly, it allows us the ability to convert a viewer into a caller.

This is not your father's method of advertising.

There are still some "old-school" lawyers who believe that it is beneath them to advertise. It is not "respectable." Those lawyers are practicing in the age of the dinosaurs. Although referral-based marketing is still the best and most profitable form of marketing, there are many lawyers and law firms who seek to boost their marketing beyond whatever referrals they get.

While it is true that you should never put all of your eggs in one basket, it is also true that if you fail to take advantage of video you will be left behind. It is becoming quite obvious that lawyers who fail to create compelling educational video are already at a significant disadvantage when trying to attract new potential clients to their law firms.

HOW SOMEONE FINDS YOUR VIDEO ONLINE

Here is the process by which somebody will go online to search for lawyer.

Remember, the psychology behind someone searching for an attorney online is critical to understand in order for you to create effective video that targets their legal problem.

- Someone with a legal problem is looking for a lawyer to help them.

- They don't know a lawyer.

- They don't know a friend or family member who knows a lawyer they could recommend.

- One of the simplest and easiest ways to begin to look for an attorney or, more importantly, to look for information about their legal problem or medical problem is to go online and type their problem into Google.

In the past, a consumer or potential client might go to the yellow pages and flip open the lawyers section and begin to call each lawyer. No longer.

Now when someone goes onto Google to look for information, they have hundreds and thousands of choices. Here are four questions to ask:

(1)   How can you stand out from the crowd?

(2) How can you gain maximum exposure?

(3) How can you maximize the chance that you will be found?

(4) How can you make your information compelling enough to actually be clicked on?

The concept of getting "found" in the search engines is a topic that would take up an entire book. Getting found has to do with optimizing how the search engines look at your content, whether written or on video. The key is having relevant useful information in multiple formats that gets the search engines to recognize that your content is highly relevant to people who are actively searching for that particular information.

Does Video Marketing Work?

TESTICULAR TORSION

A painful topic for any man.

A young child was having groin pain and was taken to an emergency room. The young doctor failed to recognize the child's testicle was twisted, and failed to timely call a pediatric surgeon to evaluate the problem. By the time the surgeon was called in and tests were done, the window of opportunity to surgically correct the problem had closed. The child lost his testicle. I created a video about this painful condition.

Every few days I get comments on this video on YouTube from people who have had this condition. It's fascinating. Viewers share their experiences and commiserate collectively with their comments.

SCAN
WITH
YOUR
**SMART
PHONE**

I received an email the other day from a gentleman who watched my video about testicular torsion. He too was experiencing pain in his groin. He did not know what to do, so he decided to reach out to me for information about his treatment options for his groin pain.

I quickly explained in a response to his comment left on YouTube that I am an attorney handling medical malpractice cases here in the state of New York. I have been in practice for more than 23 years and have relevant trial experience handling cases of improper medical care resulting in injury. I told him in plain English to go to the emergency room or to his doctor immediately!

What was so fascinating about this email that I received?

First, he found my video. Second, he watched it till the end. Third, he contacted me for more information about the content of my video.

Fourth, he asked me, an attorney, for medical advice.

There's an important, strategic lesson in that. What could be so powerful that a viewer watching my video believed that I had sufficient medical information that he would reach out and ask me medical questions?

I am not a doctor and do not portray one on TV. I do not ever pretend to be a doctor. So why would anyone ask a lawyer for medical advice? The answer may surprise you.

When you are confident and present useful information a viewer wants and needs to know, you become the go-to expert. That tip will help you greatly with your marketing.

By the way, when creating this useful content, you never have to say, "Come to me because I'm an expert at this." Instead, your viewer immediately recognizes that you have knowledge and information they need.

A PATTERN EMERGES

Are you noticing a pattern here?

What have I accomplished with the use of video? I have created an educational message that connects with my ideal viewer. They like what I have to say. They find my content compelling.

Most of the people who call my office thank me for providing them with so much information. They typically say that other attorneys simply don't provide the type of information that I do.

These videos have allowed me to stand out from the crowd and separate myself from my competitors. You can do the same.

Remember, video is simply a portal through which a message is transmitted. It is no different than TV, radio, newspaper ads, or any other media available… sort of.

The testicular torsion video came about because of a case I handled resulting in the loss of a testicle of a young boy.

Question: Why would any lawyer in their right mind create a video about testicular torsion?

The answer will reveal a marketing strategy that will open your eyes to an entirely new world.

In the testicular torsion video, I did not discuss the name of my clients nor the name of the doctor or hospital that was involved. Instead, I explained what happened to my client and why we believed that the doctor departed from good and accepted medical care. Importantly, the result that I was able to achieve for this family was insignificant for the purposes of this video.

Most attorneys reading that last statement will be confused, thinking that if they have achieved great results, then they should be talking about them on video. There is a time and place for that, but this video was not one of them.

Getting back to the question of why an attorney would create a video about some painful topic for any man viewing it, the answer is relatively simple and straightforward.

People are going online to search for information. My video provided educational information that they needed to know. That's it. Plain and simple.

WHAT DOES A VIEWER WANT TO KNOW?

My video about testicular torsion did not talk about medical malpractice cases in general. Instead, it focused on one particular medical condition that existed in one particular type of medical malpractice case that I handle. You have to understand the psychology behind what a viewer is thinking and what goes on in their mind when they search for information.

In all likelihood, the person who is looking for this information about testicular torsion is most likely a man or a parent who has questions about their own or their child's testicular torsion. They will want to know a lot of details about the condition, including how it is diagnosed and what happens in the event it is not timely diagnosed. They want that information in a concise package that doesn't preach, yell, or scream at them. They don't want to hear the words, "If you have been injured, pick up the phone and call me at 1-800-I-Sue-4-You."

DO NOT UPLOAD TO YOUTUBE
WITHOUT TAKING THESE ACTIONS

If you think that simply uploading your YouTube video will automatically make your video stand out from the crowd, you are wrong.

There are four basic steps for video. If not done correctly, you will be wasting your time and resources. Briefly, here they are:

(1) You must create a compelling headline.

(2) You must have a detailed and interesting description in the description box.

(3) You must insert relevant tags and keywords.

(4) You must have a compelling call to action at the end of your video.

In concept or theory, this is very easy to recite. Implementing it correctly is difficult for the novice video marketer. Even for the intermediate-level video marketer, there are nuances and subtleties that will drive your traffic off without you even realizing it. For the advanced marketing student, there are significant tips and strategies that are available that the majority of lawyers and video companies simply do not take advantage of.

Over the past few years I have become an avid marketing student as well as an avid video marketer. What I teach works. What I do personally to market my law practice works.

I get calls and emails every single day from people across the country asking me to help them with their legal problem. It always makes me smile when I get calls from people in other states asking for my help. Here's why.

Every one of my videos states very clearly that I am a New York medical malpractice and personal injury trial attorney.

Despite this fact, people continue to call me from California, Florida, Connecticut, Michigan, Illinois, and other states seeking my assistance. Why? Because they found the content in my video compelling enough to pick up the phone and call, regardless of the fact that I only practice in New York. While that certainly affords me the opportunity to send those cases out to other attorneys, understanding the psychology behind what motivates the viewer to pick up the phone and call is crucial.

TODAY'S EMAIL

"Mr. Oginski,

"I just watched your video on YouTube about injuries that may occur during labor and delivery, which led me to your website and now this email… it appears our son, aged 20 months is suffering from… "

This is the type of email I receive every day. Do you?

THE FACT THAT GERRY IS A SUCCESSFUL TRIAL ATTORNEY AND HAS A BOOMING PRACTICE REALLY IMPRESSED ME

"I listened to a webinar and I heard what he [Gerry] had to say. In a sense, I got to interview him in terms of video production. He was  knowledgeable, he wasn't going to have me fly to some far away studio and spend a day doing video with someone who wasn't an attorney....

Hi, I'm Greg Stokes, I'm a personal injury attorney in Atlanta, Georgia. We've been working with Gerry and his team and we've shot two sets of videos, six months apart. The second mastermind call for the next 25 videos was invaluable. Gerry has his own way of doing things and he's always right. What we did, I took copious notes, came up with 25 topics, created my 4 bullet points and then he and Harry (Gerry's partner) spent a day with me and we ripped through 25 videos. It's amazing what they can do. I believe in all this stuff, the attorney is the obstacle. What Gerry and Harry and do is they make you do it and they make you do it right. I can't tell you how great it is working with these guys.

My firm does personal injury work. We are using Gerry's Total Video Solution.

We picked Gerry because we watched him on the webinar. And for 30 minutes, he convinced me that he knew more about the subject than anybody else out there. And when he says "Total" he means total. At the end of the day, you will have produced 25 videos that you can post on your web site or you can post on your YouTube channel.

Well, I say twenty-five. Twenty-five for me and then Neil Kopitsky's doing another twenty five. These guys are tremendous. They know what they're doing. They're polished professionals. You don't have to fly away to some Hollywood studio. They'll come right to your office and work with you. You will be so satisfied, and the most important thing is they're going get you to do it, as opposed to "Oh, I've been thinking about video but I really haven't gotten a chance to do it."

I have friends that have bought their equipment for themselves, and it's still sitting in their office. Gerry won't let that happen.

Here's the reason I chose Gerry. Our marketing group had set up a webinar with him, and I got to listen to him for about 30 minutes. And what impressed me with it is he understood how video works, and even more importantly, he demonstrated how he can shoot your web site into first page ranking. You know, it's amazing that as many as

2 out of 3 people get their information from video online rather than reading your web conent. Gerry understood the process.

As far as the second mastermind call, you know it was so interesting, he worked with us, he suggested the topics, and when he came down here, we had the topics and the bullet points ready, we had exhibits that we had used in actual cases, and he pulled the whole thing together perfectly. I can't tell you how pleased I am to be schooled by Gerry and working with him. He and his team, they're fabulous. They know what they're doing, if you're thinking about getting into video, I suggest that you give them a try.

Well, you know that the fact that Gerry is a success-ful trial attorney, and he has a booming practice in Long Island really impressed me because he's out there, just like all of us, trying to get his piece of action, he's trying to get that phone to ring. And the crazy thing is if you go to lunch with Gerry, his cell phone is ringing with people that are calling from his video. The combination of a personal lawyer that tries cases and is out to keep his fair share of cases coming his way by using video convinced me to use him.

We recently got two really good cases. We tracked where they came from, the client said they had watched our YouTube videos and they were calling us because of it. To me, I'm kind of stuck in my own world and I'm always trying to break out of the box I've put myself in and it is amazing. People will call you because of the videos you post."

Greg Stokes, Esq.
Personal Injury Trial Attorney
Stokes & Kopitsky, P.A.
100 Colony Square, Suite 820
1175 Peachtree Street Northeast
Atlanta, GA 30361-6215
404-892-0014

SCAN WITH YOUR SMARTPHONE TO WATCH & LISTEN TO GREG STOKES' VIDEO.

Video Is a Portal

Video is simply a means of communicating your message to someone who's searching for it. Ten years ago, it would have been impossible to use this media to communicate these educational messages. The Internet had not yet evolved to the point where it is today. YouTube had not yet been invented, and the inventor of Facebook was still in high school.

Through the advent of YouTube and other video-sharing sites, as well as social media like Twitter, LinkedIn, and Facebook, we now have the ability to transmit messages instantly to our friends online.

Creating an entire video library has enabled me to identify and target my ideal clients and to become selective in the type of cases I choose to take. It has allowed me the ability to educate the general public. It has allowed me the ability to get viewers to know me, like me, and trust me before ever meeting me. This was unheard of before the advent of video sharing online. Instead, we had to rely on the tried and tested methods all too commonly seen in the legal marketing world.

There are still lawyers, whom I call "old school," who refuse to acknowledge or believe that video messages can dramatically improve the type of cases they get, as well as the type of leads they get. Those same lawyers believe that marketing is still beneath them and continue to rely on old-school methods of marketing their practice.

That's okay; want to know why? Because it means more cases for me and other really smart lawyers who create video to market themselves. I have long ago stopped trying to convert the nonbelievers. The only time they will recognize how important and useful video is in the marketing of law firms is when they are the last ones to create video.

There are predictions that within the next two to three years 85 percent of everything online will be video-based. This comes from online giants like Google, Yahoo, and Cisco. When your consumers are going online to search for information and they reach your website, if you don't have video, your consumers will ask, "Why not?"

As always, referrals are the best way to get new business. When someone receives a trusted recommendation from a friend or family member, that method typically outweighs all others. However, the vast majority of people who are searching for a lawyer to help them solve their legal problems do not know an attorney, since they have never been in that situation before.

How then can a consumer make an educated decision about which lawyer to choose and which one is right for them? In the days before social media and video, consumers had to rely on interruption-based marketing to learn which lawyer or law firm was right for them.

INTERRUPTION-BASED MARKETING

"Interruption-based marketing" is the term that is used to define a type of media that interrupts our daily life with a message that we simply were not looking for at that moment. An example of interruption-based media would be a television ad that comes on in the middle of your favorite show asking, "Have you been injured? If so, call the law firm of Jim Jones. We can help. Call our 800 number now."

The problem with most TV ads is that they never give the attorney an opportunity to explain to a viewer why their law firm is different from all the others who handle the same type of case. Nor do they allow the attorney to establish his expertise simply by explaining.

Most television ads for lawyers are direct marketing pieces designed to get someone to call immediately following the commercial. Although TV advertising can work really well if you put enough resources and money into your TV campaigns, the reality is that they are extremely expensive. You can spend tens of thousands of dollars just to create the commercial, and then to run it in a strategic campaign can cost you hundreds of thousands of dollars or more. I know lawyers who are spending millions of dollars a year to run their TV marketing campaigns.

What do you do as a solo practitioner or a small to midsize law firm who does not have that type of advertising budget? Can you compete with the big boys?

The more important question is: why would you want to compete?

Instead, you can do an end run around most of their marketing, and unless they are savvy online marketers, you will have beaten the pants off of them, and they won't even realize it until it's too late.

A PERFECT EXAMPLE

There is a law firm in New York that spends hundreds of thousands of dollars a year on Internet marketing. This law firm handles the same type of law that I do and competes with me for the same type of cases. They are a midsize law firm and are known to handle really good cases. Yet no matter what this law firm does online, they cannot seem to outrank me on Google.

I have it from a mutual friend that this law firm spends mid to high six figures each year with their online marketing efforts. The lawyer in charge of their marketing cannot figure out why a solo practitioner from a suburb of Manhattan continues to do better in the search engines than he does, despite all of his marketing efforts and investment of resources.

In case you did not know, if you type the words "New York medical malpractice lawyer" into Google, my website consistently comes up in the number one organic search results. Even more amazing is that I do not pay anyone a dime to make that happen. How frustrated do you think my competitor would be if he knew I didn't spend a single dime to get those results on Google? I put in time and effort, but not a dime.

Want to learn how I'm able to achieve that type of result?

The answer comes from my good friend—my webmaster guru and someone whom I consider to be a third-degree black belt in the online art of search engine optimization and websites for lawyers. His name is Tom Foster and he is the founder of FosterWebMarketing.com.

The answer is summed up in one phrase, "Content is king," and I will explain that answer in detail later on.

WHY TRADITIONAL LAWYER ADVERTISING DOESN'T WORK ON VIDEO

None of the traditional types of ads lawyers have typically used work online. Want to know why? Because none of those methods take the time to explain "Why."

Have you ever seen a newspaper ad for an attorney explain why they have information that you want to know? Have you ever seen a classified ad that has the space to explain why they are different and why they can help you instead of someone else? Have you ever seen a billboard be able to explain why you should come to them instead of their next competitor? Have you ever seen a TV ad or listened to a radio spot that takes time to explain how the information they are providing to you is different than everyone else's?

The reason why those types of advertising do not work online is because they do not take the time and do not have the ability to explain anything.

Online video on the other hand allows you unlimited time to explain things. There is no other media available that allows you to do this.

COMMUNICATION IS KEY

If communicating with clients is critical before they ever call you or come into your office, then you must optimize the way you communicate with them to maximize the chance that they will call you instead of your competitor. Written text online is a fantastic way to interact with viewers who are searching for information. The search engines love written text. However, recent studies reveal that two-thirds of adults who are online prefer to watch video over reading text. That is a very significant statistic. In order to take advantage of the majority of adults who are watching videos when searching for information, you need to create great online video content.

The problem is that most lawyer video stinks. It's not because attorneys are terrible communicators, but rather they don't understand what content their viewers want and need to know. Putting together useful information for your viewers is a multipronged approach when using video. Not only do you have to become technically proficient with the equipment, but you also have to package the material in a compelling way that gets the viewer to recognize immediately that you are confident, know your material, understand the concepts, and can transmit that to your viewer.

Your goal when creating online video is to get people to pick up the phone and call or email you. You want to be able to convert the viewer into a caller. That is your entire goal. You want your video technique to be absolutely transparent so your viewer does not become distracted. Any misstep along the way will create the chance for your viewer to doubt you.

Most of the lawyer videos that I see today have technical problems. Videos created by professional video companies do not have those technical problems, but often those attorneys are not packaging their material correctly to create a compelling message.

For the do-it-yourself attorney who is shooting video on your own, there are many challenges to getting all the video and audio settings correct. If your lighting is not correct or your frame is incorrect or there's something disturbing in the background, these will give the viewer the impression that you don't know what you're doing, and the chances of then getting them to call diminish dramatically.

The lawyer who relies on a video production company to create his video stands a much greater chance of creating good quality video. However, the real test of whether or not your video is compelling is not whether you or your family members or friends think it is a good video. The test is whether viewers pick up the phone and call you after watching those videos.

If your videos are not generating calls to your office, you must ask yourself, "Why not?" Are they fully optimized? Do they have compelling headlines? Does the description give the viewer an easy way to get in touch with you? Have the search engines recognized what your videos are about? Is the message you are conveying interesting? Is the information something that your potential clients need to know? Or rather, is it information you think they need to know?

Before I got into the video marketing arena, I never considered the psychology behind what compels someone to do something. What triggers cause a person to act?

Despite the fact that I'm a practicing trial attorney and take cases to verdict and talk to juries, I never focused on the psychology behind why jurors decide the way they do and take the action they do in their verdicts.

The only way you can become truly successful with your video marketing is to step into the shoes of your potential clients and your viewers. Only then—when you truly understand their needs, not yours—will you be able to recognize what type of information you need to create to help them.

I want you to read that paragraph again. This is a very revealing piece of information that you should pay close attention to.

The reason most lawyer video stinks is because a good number of them are still focusing on themselves.

- "I have been in practice for 25 years."

- "We have 57 years combined experience."

- "I handle the following 12 different types of law."

- "I belong to the following bar associations."

- "I graduated from XYZ law school."

Do you know that in more than 23 years of practice not a single person has ever asked me where I went to law school? Not a single person has ever asked me what bar associations I belong to. Not a single person has ever asked me or cared whether I have lectured to other attorneys about medical malpractice. Why do we attorneys believe that our credentials are so important for potential clients?

Do you really think your client is hiring you because you went to ABC law school as opposed to the XYZ law school? You really think it matters to them?

I am sure that some potential clients think your credentials are important, as they should be. We've worked hard to achieve our credentials and our successes and experiences in our careers. We should all be proud of them. However, the majority of potential clients who are looking for an attorney online do not care about us. They don't care where we went to law school. They don't care what associations we belong to. They don't care what country clubs we belong to. They don't care what cars we drive. They don't care what awards we have received.

The only thing they do care about is that we have the experience to help them solve their legal problem. That's it. They do not care about you or me. The only common concern among our potential clients who are looking for us online is whether we have the knowledge and expertise necessary to help solve their legal problem. The reason they are coming to you is because they like what they see, they like what they hear, and they believe they can trust you.

Trust plays a huge role in getting an online viewer to pick up the phone and call you. If you are unable to generate trust through your online communications, you will never get that call.

When I say "online communications," I'm talking about information that gives them a taste to recognize that you have more information that they need to know. That is why online video marketing works so well. It shows the viewer in striking color, right in front of them—as opposed to telling about it, you are actually showing them—that you have the information they need.

You are not selling anything to them. You are not pitching something to them. You are not boasting; you're being 100 percent truthful, 100 percent honest. You're being 100 percent ethical and are taking the time to teach and educate your online viewer.

How many of your competitors do the same?

If you take the time to teach and educate, you will clearly set yourself apart from all of your colleagues and competitors.

Again, do not misinterpret my words. When I say educate and teach, I do not mean that you are giving a mini-CLE lecture. You are not going to take 10 minutes to explain some arcane area of law. Your potential client simply does not care about that. You are the solutions man or woman. You have the answers. Our clients come to us because we know what to do. They don't care how we do it, they only care that we have the answers to help them solve their problems.

Our clients do not care what paperwork we actually have to file to get the lawsuits started. They don't care what a motion for summary judgment is. They don't care about a lot of the minutia that you must deal with in handling their day-to-day case. Instead, they just want someone to help them achieve the results they need.

BUILDING A RELATIONSHIP

How do you build a relationship online? The point was hammered home in a blog post from my good friend Dave Lorenzo, a legal marketing expert. He discussed how crucial it is to establish a relationship when building your law firm. He emphasized that there is no magic silver bullet. Rather, the process begins with a simple relationship that focuses on the client, their problems, and the solutions you can offer.

Without relationship, there is no trust. Without trust, the client becomes dissatisfied and fraught with fear.

How then can you build trust and a strong relationship with your potential clients without ever meeting them or speaking to them? The answer is simple.

With video. There is no other form of communication available that we as attorneys can use to build a relationship, trust, and likability before ever meeting that client.

Think about how you communicate with your friends online. Maybe you'll begin a conversation on Facebook or a blog, or offer your thoughts and opinions about somebody else's comment or post. Maybe you'll join in the conversation on Twitter. The problem with that method of communication is that it is unnatural. It takes a very long time to build up credibility with a group of people who are following that particular conversation.

Online marketers recognize the value of promoting this type of relationship, and I heartily agree. However, there is a better way to communicate with your online viewers. It is creating video—basically as a conversation with your viewers. Admittedly, it is not a conversation yet; however, there is nothing else online that is better for establishing a relationship and trust.

I have new clients who come into the office telling me, "Mr. Oginski, I feel like I already know you ... I want you to handle my case." These people tell me daily that they have watched many of my videos. That's how powerful this medium is.

Lawyers who recognize the important value of building relationships also recognize how crucial video is to marketing their law firm. Those attorneys tend to develop the strongest and most loyal clients because of the personal relationships they have developed from day one.

Thanks to Dave Lorenzo for reminding us of how important this basic concept is.

I WANTED SOMEBODY WHO KNEW WHAT I WAS TALKING ABOUT. A LAWYER, NOT JUST A VIDEO PERSON.

"Hi. My name is Steven Hamilton. I'm a board certified criminal defense attorney in Lubbock, Texas and this is a testimonial for Gerry and the Lawyers Video program.

We spent about an hour together and it really gave me a good idea of brainstorming on what we wanted to do or what I wanted to try and do in the video clips. In that point in time, I knew I had talked to you on the phone, we had talked about your program, I did a lot of research on it before I decided to go further. But you gave me a good feeling that, quite frankly Gerry, that you knew what you were talking about.

And you were giving me ideas in how do we get this information out in an educational format. Not a sales pitch because that's not what I do. But how can I communicate to people about issues that I think will be important to them. And you helped me chop that up.

I've done a lot of research and I have a good Internet presence and the rankings are fairly high these days. But a lot of the issues show that video really is the way of communication. I tell people every day that we live in a 140 characters society and I just thought videos would be easier for clients. Especially when they're really worried they can sort of get to know me a little bit, see me, try to get my philosophy and get a good feeling before they came into the office so I can bond with them.

I wanted to get a camera and just film it myself, and try to figure out how to cut it and put it up on YouTube. And then I got an email, found you and really started looking at it and studying it and realized I probably shouldn't do it if it wasn't going to be good quality. I was concerned that if people thought it was just somebody sitting on their back porch doing it, that it would actually hurt instead of help build credibility.

So, you spent the time with me Gerry. You talked to me about it. I never felt a hard sales pitch. Now the fact that you're a practicing lawyer and you're doing this as well, that was big to me. It says to me "Look, I'm just not a guy out there with a camera trying to sell somebody this. This is what I do."

You know, I think you have a lot of credibility, that's what I decided. And if I was going to go with somebody, I wanted somebody who knew what I was talking about. A lawyer, not just a video person to come in and shoot a lot of video to put it up on the website.

Well, you spent a lot of time with me in the mastermind call. You also gave me some homework assignments. I would say I tried to do that homework assignment. I knew that we were investing significant time and financially there was a cost to it, so I didn't want you to come in and for me not to be prepared. So, I did my homework. I got all the questions together and I practiced. I felt confident that I knew what I was talking about but I was really nervous on how the whole system was going to work and how many times we were going to have to start and stop and go through the whole process and the feeling of whether or not it would be worth the investment that we were putting into it.

I think your system is great. A couple of days before you got here all the stuff arrives and I just leave it in the boxes. Then you come in and you put it all together and show me how to work it. But I'm not responsible during the video shoot. You have great staff here. It was very soothing for me as far as the confidence building as we went through the day and you gave great feedback and great ideas.

We'd shoot some things over but you also – you're a very positive person, so there was a lot of positive reinforcement making me feel good about what we were doing. Not in a sales pitch way, but I'm actually accomplishing something that's going to look good, be educational, and help my clients. I think we shot at least 50 videos in one day, which to me was amazing. That was probably the thing I was most nervous about when you said we were going to shoot 50 videos, I thought we would be here until midnight and it's well short of midnight when we finished. So I'm really pleased with the amount of work that we got done in one day.

I would say call Gerry. He'll spend the time with you on the phone to talk to you about what he does. It's not a hard sell. He's not telling you "Gee, you have to do this and I'm better than everybody else." And then if you decide to go forward on it, he gives you some options. He gave me time to think about it and I didn't sign up the very first time I talked to Gerry. I needed to go back and digest it and think about things and I could call him back and he would spend his time — at that point in time with no investment from me in the case. So there is credibility with you Gerry and I am very pleased in working through the video."

Stephen Hamilton, Esq.
Criminal Defense Attorney
802 Main Street
Lubbock, TX 79401
(806) 794-0394

SCAN WITH YOUR SMARTPHONE TO WATCH & LISTEN TO STEPHEN HAMILTON' VIDEO.

Quality Counts

When deciding to create educational video to market your law firm online, you must keep in mind the following overriding message: *your viewer believes that the quality of your video is somehow correlated with your legal ability.*

Of course, your viewer is not qualified to accurately evaluate the quality of your legal services simply by watching a video. However, with the abundance of video that gets uploaded to YouTube and other video-sharing sites on a daily basis, viewers tend to be hypercritical. They get distracted easily. A video that is not technically proficient loses the opportunity to engage their viewer forever.

The reality is that there are many excellent lawyers putting up really bad video. One of the biggest problems that do-it-yourself lawyers have is that they listen to "marketing gurus" who simply tell them to buy inexpensive video equipment, press the red record button, and directly upload to YouTube without editing. If a quick and dirty video is what you intend to create, then in all likelihood that is the type of client you can expect to attract.

A FAST-FOOD VIDEO

I critiqued an attorney video not long ago of a lawyer who was shooting video in his car while driving. He pulled into a fast-food restaurant take-out lane and said to the camera, "Hold on just a second." He then turned to the woman at the drive-through and placed his order. He waited until his food was given to him and his transaction finished. "Have a nice day" is what you heard from the fast-food employee through the tinny speaker. He put his car in drive and then turned back to the camera and continued his message. He then uploaded that video to YouTube… without editing any of it out.

If you're interested in his content, do you really want to see the lawyer at the drive-through? Is that the type of message you want to send to your ideal client?

Always remember who your educational message is geared to. Think about what they are looking for when they go online to search for information about their legal problems.

USING YOUR ADORABLE KIDS IN YOUR VIDEO

In another video I critiqued, a lawyer used his adorable kids as props. Then he badmouthed another lawyer in his town.

What's the problem with that?

First, there was no reason to have the kids in the video. Second, the lawyer disparaged a competing lawyer. Really bad move. That type of video will get you in front of the grievance committee and likely subject you to a libel and slander claim as well.

THE NOISY COFFEE SHOP VIDEO

Imagine sitting in a coffee shop with poor lighting. The music is blaring in the background. Customers are coming and going. The noise level is high. Picture an attorney sitting on a worn couch in this café using his laptop to create video. He's using his webcam and the camera is staring up into his nose. His voice is barely above a whisper. He's trying to give useful information.

Do you think this video will attract his ideal clients? This type of video comes from a real attorney. He creates lots of these videos in this venue. I can't understand how anyone would come to him based on his videos.

You would think this would be common sense. However, having reviewed thousands of attorney videos, I can tell you *with certainty* that really good lawyers put crappy videos online and don't even realize what they've done.

Learning how to create compelling video has *nothing* to do with the technical components involved or the mechanics of shooting your video and getting it onto your computer to begin the editing process.

Let me say that again.

Great compelling video has nothing to do with the equipment. We all have basically the same equipment… sort of. The difference is understanding how to use what you have to make excellent video.

CASE STUDIES

While lecturing recently to a group of really smart attorneys at a legal marketing seminar in Pennsylvania, I showed them 10 videos. I downloaded those videos from YouTube just two weeks before my lecture. They were all created by really intelligent attorneys who were trying desperately to create great quality video to market their law firms.

My audience was treated to a video bonanza. The videos were awful. It was, however, entertaining for teaching purposes, and illustrated the point that these lawyers don't understand how to combine good video technique with a compelling message.

How compelling can an attorney video be when your background has horns behind you which appear to be coming out of your head? It's true!

One video showed an attorney referring to himself in the third person the entire video. That was bizarre.

Another video was of an attorney standing on the beach after coming back from court. The attorney did not use an external microphone and had no idea the wind would affect his video.

The wind totally obliterated everything he had to say.

What was amazing was that he put that video online to market his practice. Here's the other amazing thing. There is no way this lawyer listened to his video first before he uploaded it. Had he bothered to spend a moment to listen to his video, he would have immediately recognized it was a horrible video and deleted it immediately.

DO YOU REALLY KNOW EVERYTHING ABOUT CREATING VIDEO?

As lawyers, we believe we know it all. We think it's so easy when someone says to go out and buy equipment that is simple to use. It is simple if you're using it to create home videos of your kids and your family. However, if you want to create the impression that you are an excellent attorney, then you better make sure that the quality of your video is excellent. Your viewer demands high-definition video that has great quality.

Your viewer demands a video that is framed well, is properly lit, and has great audio. Those are the basics. If you make a video that does not communicate all of those technical requirements, my recommendation is to ditch the video and hire a video marketing company to create great video for you.

WE WOULD HAVE BEEN LOST WITHOUT GERRY'S DIRECTION

Michael & Ryan McGlinn
McGlinn & McGlinn, Juvenile Law Center

"I believe the reason we chose video is it appears as if our society is wanting video. They're used to video now, they want video in terms of trying to convince them to use a particular person or service. Seeing the person is worth a thousand words. As a picture is worth a thousand words, I think a video is worth more. And, people aren't just going to read what's on a static website. They'll go through a couple lines, I think. And maybe they'll look at results or something like that.

I think they want to see a video of people. We were questioning whether we wanted to do videos, was it worth it cost wise. I was searching on the Internet for videos for lawyers and I saw your site, Gerry and looked at what you had to say and your being an attorney; it seemed to be a passion for you in addition to your own work. And a willingness to educate other attorneys how to use the video medium to assist them in their marketing. That's what led me to contacting you.

Well, the main thing was that we had a phone session with you and you broke it down in some literature about key issues that you need to look at: you need to look at in your practice, what are common questions that you routinely get from people on the phone.

So we sat down together and started brainstorming between the two of us as to what are the issues that are normally presented to us. What are the common phone calls we get all the time from clients? What are the real hotbed issues that we think clients are going to want to hear about? That's kind of how we came up with an outline of topics for videos we thought would be useful.

Well, I felt completely unprepared — like I didn't know what I was doing. And it was a rough start, let's put it that way. But gradually as we went through the day, it got a little more comfortable and I hope it turned out all right. I'm sure at the very beginning, the editing will — there will be a great deal of editing required for those initial videos. There was definitely a progression where you started to feel more comfortable. You started to understand what the idea was behind the videos; how to introduce a topic and how to personalize it and put yourselves in the shoes of someone wanting to watch the video.

You started to grasp the idea, grasp those concepts, and it started to flow a lot easier. You're able to kind of seamlessly transition to introduction, to exiting, to content.

Gerry, the other thing I wanted to mention about videos is I have wanted since probably a year ago to get the message out on some of the points we mentioned in our videos to families, to educate them about certain things about protecting their children from pornography. Fathers who are helping raise their kids, co-parents or divorced fathers, from getting into trouble or getting accusations against them, families losing their kids and their families because of accusations. I'm hoping somebody someday will see some of these videos and it will be a benefit to them.

We don't have the technological savvyness to do it on our own. We needed the assistance of someone who knew what they were doing. We can spend probably 10 times the amount of time today, creating 2 videos – let alone 50. So, I think when it boils down to it having someone like yourself who knows what they're doing, has a system in place, and can really kind of work with you to get the videos flowing, get the content going, it's definitely the way to go. I think you'd spend just too much time, too much energy, in trying to do it yourself.

Maybe at some point in the future, maybe years from now, we understand this process a lot more. But initially to get going, this is definitely the way to go.

The other thing, Gerry, we did look at your website. We're extremely impressed by what you've done. Not only videos, but your books, your blog and what you had to say.

We did have an offer to do videos and I think we would have been lost without Gerry's direction, what to hit on, what not to say. He's an attorney and he's a marketer par excellence. I know he works at it and he joins other groups who talk about marketing. We feel like we got a pro to assist us here, and it's well worth the money."

Michael McGlinn, Esq.
Juvenile Criminal Defense Attorney
McGlinn & McGlinn, Attorneys at Law
5030 Camino de la Siesta, Suite 350
San Diego, CA 92108
Phone: 619-291-5115

CHAPTER 9

SCAN WITH YOUR SMARTPHONE TO WATCH & LISTEN TO MICHAEL & RYAN MCGLINN'S VIDEO.

Seven Reasons Not to Create Video

1. PERSONAL REFERRALS

We all know that personal referrals are the best and most trusted source for new business. Assuming that you have a trusted referral network who already knows you and loves you, then you don't need to create video to market to your referral sources.

Assuming for the moment that you have a devoted group of followers who eagerly send you new cases on a regular basis and that you don't want any more new cases, then by all means do not create video.

2. TV ADS

If your TV advertising is bringing in so much profitable work that you do not need any additional cases, then it goes without saying you should not be creating video to market your practice online. Simply continue to pay tons of money to produce and air your commercials on the same time slots. If your ROI (return on your investment) is good with your TV ads, then you do not need online video.

3. YELLOW PAGES

If you are one of the few lawyers who are still using the yellow pages and are getting good results, then you do not need to create video to market your practice. If you have found one successful way to market your law firm, you certainly don't want to create additional revenue streams. Why would you do that?

It is good that you are relying solely on an outdated and outmoded means of communication to get more potential clients. Hopefully, you will be able to grow your business exponentially as the yellow pages continue to become less and less relevant every day.

4. NETWORKING

If you go to legal networking events three to four times a week, then you are likely getting tons of calls and referrals from your networking sources. In that case, you certainly wouldn't want to create video to market your practice since you are generating lots of business from your networking.

I do have an important question though. Does your networking work in the middle of the night? Does it work when you are on vacation? Does it work on the weekends when you're not at a networking event?

What happens if you are unable to reciprocate with people whom you have just met at a networking event? Will they still continue to send you leads?

5. YOU HAVE AN ONLINE PRESENCE

Congratulations! You, along with millions of other lawyers in the United States, have a website. When you created your website you must have thought that you were the only lawyer around with such a beautifully designed online brochure. Of course, your website is unique.

I am sure you have great content that you update on a frequent, consistent basis. I'm also sure that your search engine optimization (SEO) experts have enabled you to maintain excellent placement in the search engines.

I have some important questions for you. How many people who actually come to your website become paying clients? How long do they stay on your website? When they call your office, do they tell you how much they love the information on your website and that they feel as if they've gotten to know you, like you, and trust you from photographs of a courthouse, a flag, or a gavel? If the answer is yes, then you probably do not need to create video to market your already successful online practice.

6. YOU ALREADY HAVE VIDEO

If you have five videos, why would you want to create 50 more? Why would you ever want to create 100 more? What could more videos possibly do to help you market your law firm?

I'm sure that every time someone does a search for your legal specialty, all five of your videos show up on the first page of results. I'm sure that your five videos are doing so remarkably well that everybody who calls your office has viewed all five of your videos and decided unequivocally that you are the only lawyer for them.

I'm sure that the content you created in those videos is so compelling that everybody who starts to watch your videos becomes a caller.

In all likelihood, you have created those videos on your own. Good for you. You're a renegade. You understand technology and the hundreds of steps involved in creating great quality video that is properly formatted, edited, search-engine opti-mized, and distributed online. You must have lots of time on your hands to be able to do all that. Wonderful.

Since you are a do-it-yourselfer, you don't need any more video. It's up online and you're done. Maybe next year you'll create another five videos.

7. YOU DON'T BELIEVE THAT PEOPLE WATCH VIDEO

You also don't believe that anyone in their right mind would pick up the phone to call a lawyer after watching a lawyer video. Besides, nobody watches video online anyway.

If that conclusion is based on anecdotal stories from your colleagues, then obviously you do not want to create video to market your practice. It is a wise move not to confirm those statements for yourself and do your own due diligence to see whether those comments by your colleagues in the lawyer's lounge are in fact true.

Of course, you will only do the type of marketing that your fellow attorneys do, that you learn about through word of mouth, because copying other lawyers and what they do is the most successful way to market your practice.

CONCLUSION

If you fit into any one or more categories listed above, then you do not want to create video to market your practice. In fact, you would be wasting your time, resources, and marketing budget to do so. Instead, let those other attorneys go ahead and do something foolish like marketing their law firms online using video. That's perfectly okay, and in fact I recommend it if you see yourself in any one of these seven categories.

THE FACT THAT GERRY OGINSKI IS AN ATTORNEY GIVES YOU THE PERSPECTIVE THAT HE'S IN THE SAME BOAT YOU ARE.

"Hi, my name is Joe Hanyon. I'm a partner in the law firm of Merwine, Hanyon & Kaspszyk. We have offices in northeast Pennsylvania and it's primarily my responsibility to market the firm and come up with new ideas on how to expand the firm and make sure we have a good, steady supply of great clients. In my quest to market our firm and to let people know about our services, I travel the country and attend various seminars on the law and on marketing law firms throughout the country. You know, there's lots of ideas floating out there on how to market a small firm like ours and I met Gerry Oginski at an ATLAS marketing seminar in Naples, Florida.

I met Gerry at a marketing seminar this past winter in March of 2011 and at that particular seminar, there's lots of great ideas on how to market a law firm. But I was particularly attracted to the manner in which the Lawyers' Video Studio had planned to get your firm noticed on the web and noticed in video and YouTube. I found Gerry's approach to be a common sense approach to what people are looking for. It's not necessarily what we think our video should be, it's really what people are searching for.

Gerry has made a study of how people search the web and what they need from lawyers and then he's able to communicate that to the lawyers who are delivering their content on video. And that's what I really found intriguing is the methodology by which we shoot the videos and the way that he communicates that methodology.

You know, before we started shooting the video today, we had a couple of calls from Gerry to talk about how to really prepare for the videos. We're polished professionals to some extent, but we're just not used to being in front of a camera and making videos. He walked us through that process.

In that process I also went on the Web and looked at some of Gerry's videos and looked at videos of others and tried to understand what is really compelling about video. When he came here today we didn't know how we would perform. What was interesting was Gerry's coaching method and the way he makes you feel relaxed and makes you understand what you have to do in front of the camera.

It's now the latter part of the day, we've been shooting here since 8 o'clock today and we're still actually shooting more video as I'm talking to you right now and I think it's gone great. We can't wait for Gerry to give us our first set of edits and upload this on our video channel and get us out there on the Web.

You know, it's just like doing anything. When you start the video process, there's a lot of things you just aren't aware of that slowly you become aware of. As you become aware of them, you forget about how you have to do them so you can focus on the substance of what you have to say. Throughout the day we actually became more and more comfortable, and some of us who we thought wouldn't do great on video actually were the best performers and it was amazing.

You know, the fact that Gerry Oginski is an attorney, obviously gives you some kinship with him but it gives you the perspective that he's in the same boat you are. He's out there competing in a very, very competitive market.

He understands what it is to be an attorney and what it is to try to communicate what you know to the clients. I think that was invaluable. I don't think that if we hired another crew to come in here, or someone who wasn't involved in the law, that our content and the way that the video is delivered would have been the quality of what we hope we ended up with.

You know, the first thing, it's funny how you start realizing that emotionalism is just about involved in all the purchases that you have, and your ability to have a rapport with people when you're working with them is important. The thing about working with Gerry is that it was worth just hanging out with Gerry and hopefully making him a friend for life. If we end up getting a couple of good videos out of it, that's just a bonus. The main thing is just making a real good friend.

You have to feel comfortable with the people you're working with and Gerry's comfort level and his interpersonal skills really come through right away. I think that is going to reflect in the quality of our videos and the type of clients that end up contacting us, for the benefit of the firm."

Joe Hanyon, Esq.
Personal Injury & Disability Lawyer
MHK Attorneys
2642 Rt. 940
Pocono Summit, PA 18360
Phone: (570) 839-8050
Toll Free: (855) MHK-ATTY

SCAN WITH YOUR SMARTPHONE TO WATCH & LISTEN TO JOE HANYON'S VIDEO.

You Must Understand Your Viewer

Do not skip this chapter because you think it's all psychobabble. This is critical. There are psychological triggers that cause someone to watch a video and then to pick up the phone and call you. If you fail to understand this concept, you will lose the ability to maximize the chances that someone will come to you instead of your colleague.

Go back to our goal for creating video. Our sole purpose to create an educational message using video is to get someone to recognize that we have information they want. It is to get them to recognize that they can trust us. It is to give them a little taste of the information we have.

I will say it again, your viewer does not care about the arcane area of law that you practice. Instead, they only want the results you can achieve for them.

First, you must convince your viewer that you have information that they need. The only way to do that is to understand what information they truly need as opposed to information you are trying to give them. Most lawyers do not understand that distinction. Most lawyers who create video think that what they say is all-important; how could anybody not watch what they have to say in a video?

If you make your videos all about you, your viewer will leave, never to come back. Remember what I said earlier. Your viewer does not care about you or your credentials. Maybe if you are general counsel looking specifically for someone who graduated from Harvard Law School and clerked for a federal judge and are now deciding between two equally credentialed lawyers, then that may be a consideration.

However, for the most part, your viewer only wants to see and hear information they are looking for. I will say it again. Step into the shoes of your viewer.

As a trial attorney, that phrase is taboo when speaking to a jury. We are never permitted to ask a jury to step into the shoes of our injured plaintiff. Although ideally that is exactly what we want them to do, we must beat around the bush to get them to peer into our client's life in order for them to visualize what our injured client must live with for the rest of their life.

CAN YOU VISUALIZE YOUR IDEAL CLIENT?

Let's say you handle real-estate transactions. Your ideal client is someone who has a real-estate dispute or a contract dispute. What type of content do you think you could create that would compel a business owner with a contract dispute to call you?

How about "Five things business owners need to know when their vendor fails to live up to their contract"?

Maybe you create a video titled "You just put down a $30,000 deposit on a home and someone steals it out from under you. Can you recover your deposit?"

The titles I just listed are just two examples of what your ideal client would be looking for if they were in that situation. That should trigger lots of ideas in your mind about the type of content you can create to generate interest for your viewers. This is a very powerful strategy that I teach in my Total Online Video Marketing Program to attorneys who create video with me.

Not only do you have to understand what your viewers are going through, but you also have to understand the psychology behind creating compelling headlines. You also need to know how to create an interesting description, what keywords to use, and how to package your content to make your information interesting and compelling.

As someone who has been doing this for many years now, I will tell you this is no easy task. It's like telling a lawyer right out of law school to go try a complex contract dispute between IBM and Microsoft. Sure, the lawyer learned basic trial techniques in law school, but having never tried a case in his life, do you think he's going to be well prepared going up against law firms with litigators who have 20 years of experience?

As one of my mentors used to say, "Nobody is born a great trial attorney. It is something that you learn and only comes with practice and experience." The same is true for creating compelling video.

You can learn how to do all this on your own and do it through trial and error. You can do it while practicing law; handling cases; putting out client fires; and dealing with motions, meetings, depositions, and everything else that goes along with your practice area. Or you can hire an experienced video marketing company to help you do this.

MOTIVATING TRIGGERS

What actually motivates a viewer searching online for an attorney to pick up the phone and call you?

It might be the way we look. It might be the way we sound. We might offer more information than our competitor. Maybe our competitors have only static websites without any video. On the other hand, maybe they do have video and the quality of their video is nowhere near as good as yours. Maybe their message is inadequate. Maybe their videos do not connect with the viewer as yours do.

The primary motivating factor is either pleasurable gain or fear of pain. With video marketing, your online viewer is not going to search and find your content for pleasurable gain. Why not?

It is not entertaining. It will not make them laugh. It will not take their mind off their problems. Your videos will do none of that. Nobody is searching for an attorney video for enjoyment… unless of course they are a masochist for watching dull, boring videos.

YouTube does not have a category of "Click here to watch boring attorney video." You need to get rid of the notion that people will watch your video because you're such a handsome guy.

Instead, the majority of your viewers are in search of that magic pill that will make them feel better. They want a solution to their horrible legal problem. They are in pain, both figuratively and in reality. They fear more pain and are searching online for someone to help take away the pain. Take away their troubles. Ease their fears.

An online viewer wants someone to guide them and teach them. Fear of pain is a very powerful motivating factor. Think about it. When you have a toothache, you go to the dentist to relieve the excruciating pain. When you have surgery, an anesthesiologist puts you to sleep to avoid feeling pain. The pharmaceutical companies make billions of dollars a year making pain reliever pills. To take away your pain.

Knowing what pain points your ideal client has is key to understanding what content to create that triggers a call. Always look to their pain.

What can you do to take away their pain? To solve their legal pain? To alleviate their suffering?

You must show your viewer the solution to relieve their pain is to pick up the phone to call you.

But wait a second…

I envision some lawyer reading this will create a video that says, "If you're in pain, pick up the phone and call me right now." No, no, no. Do *not* do that. That is not what I mean. Let me give you a concrete example.

Mom just saw Dad bleed to death when his dialysis shunt ruptured. The autopsy report said Dad's death was due to erosion of the fistula where the needle was inserted for dialysis. Mom has dire pressing questions about how this could happen. Daughter has questions about how a doctor or dialysis center could not recognize this problem.

Where's the "pain" here?

It's not the mental anguish they're suffering. That's too simple and ineffective to gain their attention. It's their lack of knowledge and information. They need answers. They can't understand how and why this could have happened. That's their "pain."

What should you do once you have truly identified their pain points? The answer is right in front of you. Start creating content that addresses their pain.

Stop. Do not use cliché marketing phrases like "Has your loved one been injured in an accident? Are you looking for answers? If so, pick up the phone and call…" *No, no, no.* That is not a compelling reason for someone to call. Stop using the same nonsense call to action. It doesn't work with online video.

Instead, create video that describes what a fistula is. Teach your viewer how a dialysis fistula can rupture. Explain to your viewer what happens when it ruptures and how little time it takes for the body to bleed to death.

I want to you reread that paragraph again and again. It contains a million-dollar strategy that I regularly use and teach my video marketing clients. The content in that type of video directly addresses their pain points. It speaks to them. It teaches them. It educates them. Those are motivating factors.

When you teach and educate a viewer who is in search of pain relief, you are viewed as the go-to expert who has the solution they are looking for. You are the pain reliever!

These psychological insights should be applied to all your marketing efforts and not just video.

WHY VIEWERS NEED TO SEE AND HEAR YOU

Earlier I said that the majority of viewers online prefer to watch video instead of reading text. The majority of lawyers today still have text-based websites. Most attorney websites are static and frankly boring. We have come a long way in a short period of time from when our websites were originally nothing more than four or five pages of a law firm brochure with our Martindale-Hubble listing. Lawyer directories used to be the rage five and six years ago. Most of those have fallen out of favor today.

Lawyer directories did nothing to distinguish one lawyer from another. Paying a premium to be placed higher on a directory listing did very little to set you apart from everyone else. Seven and eight years ago, search engines placed lawyer directories highly. Now, you'd be lucky if you find one or two.

Since video is so prevalent online, a viewer who goes online to search for information *expects* to see you on video. If you do not put compelling educational video on your website and other places online, your consumers will question why you are not on video. They will not give it a lot of thought. They will quickly realize that you do not have video and often will click away, never to return.

I say this not to scare you but to get you to recognize how vital and important it is to create video to market your practice today. In the next chapter I'm going to show you what will happen if you do not create video to market your law firm.

WHY DID I CHOOSE GERRY OGINSKI? WELL, QUITE FRANKLY, I DECIDED TO GO TO THE BEST.

"Hi. This is Troy Rosasco, from Turley, Redmond, Rosasco & Rosasco here in New York. We're disability lawyers. Why did I decide to use Gerry Oginski and the Lawyers Video Studio?

Well, quite frankly, I'm a big follower of the internet and I know that Lawyers Video is the wave of the future. Put in any search term into the Internet today and up comes a couple of videos. I saw some of my competitors doing it and I knew I had to do it too.

Why did I choose Gerry Oginski? Well, quite frankly, I decided to go to the best. If I'm going to be out there on the Internet and people are going to see me for a long time, I wanted to get a real professional here with real high quality videos.

The good thing about Gerry is a couple of things. Number one: We had a coaching session before we even looked into the camera. We talked about our strategy as to what we wanted to gain out of the videos and how to do it. Then, when the day came to do the videos, my 3 partners and I did 50 videos all in one day. Now, I know that sounds almost impossible but it's possible with Gerry.

Why? Because he was right behind the camera helping us and coaching us all the way. He really is a pro. There's no question in my mind that these videos are going to help in our overall marketing campaign, in our overall Internet strategy, and I encourage you if you're interested in lawyer video to talk to Gerry Oginski. He really is a pro."

Troy Rosasco, Esq.
Social Security Disability & Workers Compensation Attorney
Turley, Redmond, Rosasco & Rosasco
3075 Veterans Memorial Highway
Ronkonkoma, New York 11779
Phone: 631.582.3700

SCAN WITH YOUR SMARTPHONE TO WATCH & LISTEN TO TROY ROSASCO'S VIDEO.

Do or Die

I will be the first to say it now. Your law firm will be obsolete soon if you do not embrace video now.

You think I'm kidding right? You think this is a "gloom and doom" message, right? Wrong. It's a wake-up call.

In the 1960s, vinyl phonograph records were heavily used and everyone felt they'd be around forever.

In the 70s, 8-track players were all the rage.

Cassette tapes then came on the scene and made 8-track players obsolete. Everyone thought cassette tapes would be around forever.

Then came CDs and, slowly but surely, cassette tapes went the same way as the dinosaurs.

Rotary dial phones used to be the standard … way back when.

Then came push-button phones.

How many rotary phones do you see now? None.

You see where this is going, right?

In the 70s, law firms used carbon paper to make multiple copies. Does anyone use carbon paper now? Typewriters were all the rage. Remember those huge IBM Selectric typewriters? You rarely see them now. Computers rule. Do you know any law firm that doesn't use computers?

For 30 years, yellow pages were the source for people looking for an attorney. How many of you still use the yellow pages to market your law firm?

You have a website, right? Why?

I'll answer that for you: to stay ahead of the curve. Everyone else started getting websites, and you wisely recognized that you needed one too. Besides, it's got a great return on investment. How many lawyers do you know today who do *not* have a website? Virtually none.

If you were a prospective client and went online to find an attorney, only to realize that the lawyer you were looking for didn't have a website, you would want to know why.

Here's an undisputed fact: Pew Research did a recent study that showed 66 percent of adults who go online prefer to watch video than read text. 33 percent prefer text. That's twice as many people looking for video.

YOU SNOOZE, YOU LOSE

Again, why did you create a website? Because other lawyers were using new technology to "get their name out there," right? You didn't want to be left behind. Why did you join Facebook? Everybody was doing it, and you realize it's not just hype to be on FB. The social implications are huge. Same for Twitter and LinkedIn.

You did these things because you probably saw other lawyers doing it too, and you didn't want to be left behind.

When lawyers first started putting their info onto websites, they had no idea what to do with it. Blogs were unheard of. In fact, people called them "diaries." When I first heard the term "blog," I couldn't understand why anyone would post personal comments about their daily activities online. It just didn't make sense.

Now, there are millions of blogs. Each one fighting for online space. When YouTube came on the scene less than six years ago, nobody could figure out how to get video from a camera and upload it online. Smart lawyers tried to put their TV commercials onto YouTube thinking somebody must want to watch it. Let's just throw it up there and see what happens.

In the early days of online video, bandwidth was very expensive. Video file size was extremely limited. As technology evolved, uploading video became easier, and video-sharing sites started accepting larger and larger video files. Initially, YouTube couldn't figure out how to monetize their videos.

Well, along comes a little search-engine company with a funky sounding name (Google) that buys the blossoming video-sharing site called YouTube for over a *billion* dollars!

Next thing you know, YouTube is the #2 search engine in the world, and *millions of videos are viewed daily.*

So, let's go back to my original question. "Why did you create a website?" To attract viewers and to show how you're right for someone looking for a lawyer. Yet there are now millions of lawyer websites online. How do you stand out from all of your competitors online? "We care." "We have nicer pictures and graphics." "We have flash animation." "We are experts at what we do."

Yes, that's nice. But how do you "show" your viewers that you're different?

The answer is with video. (As if you didn't know that's what I'd say.) Seriously. Your online viewers expect you to have video. They want to see you. They want to hear you. They want to listen to what you have to say: Are you intelligent? Do you have a deep voice? Are you wearing nice clothes? What does your office look like? Do you have an understanding of the type of legal problem I have?

The only true way to answer these questions is with video.

My prediction is that lawyers who do not adapt to their consumers' wants and desires will not only lose business to their competitors, but will become obsolete in a short time.

Remember, potential clients searching for an attorney online will compare you to other lawyers online. If you don't have information they want, in the media they want, they will go elsewhere. That's a fact.

TOP 10 REASONS WHY SOLO AND SMALL-FIRM LAWYERS SHOULD HAVE VIDEOS

1. Viewers get to see you.

2. They get to hear you.

3. They get to know you.

4. They begin to trust you before they ever meet you.

5. They beg you to take their case.

6. You no longer have to sell yourself to your prospective clients.

7. No other marketing media allows you to create a message one time and have it played 10 times, 10,000 times, or 1 million times—all for the same exact cost of zero.

8. Nothing else allows you the ability to target your high-value, high-target clients.

9. Establish your expertise without ever having to say you're an expert.

10. Adapt to new technology or risk becoming obsolete.

THE BOTTOM LINE

Your consumers—your prospective clients and current clients—expect you to be on video. It's no longer an option. Google and Cisco predict that within two to three years, the majority of online content will be video. If you do not embrace video and adapt and accept the opportunity you have now to change, you and your law firm will be as obsolete as the 8-track player and cassette tapes. Guaranteed.

I THINK YOU DID AN EXCELLENT JOB

"I'm Scott Harford, I'm an attorney with Lynch Daskal Emery in New York City. We had an initial meeting with Gerry, and I remember I was initially a little hesitant to do this since it can be nerve-racking. He said, "This is how you're going to prepare. You're going to do a general outline and at the end of the day, you're not going to look at that outline. You know your cases and you're going to be able to look at the camera, talk about your cases with no outline at all because you know this stuff and you know it cold.

You are going to talk just like you would talk to anybody else. You have to get comfortable in front of a camera and it's going to take time and effort and you have to be prepared. When I come to your office to shoot video, I expect you to be prepared."

In my particular instance, the way I prepared was I had an outline which was going to be shown to me during the filming. Before I even started, Gerry told me "You're not even going look at it. You're just going speak. You know this stuff. Talk to the camera and tell them. Tell them as if you're talking to a friend."

What happened? Why are you in the wrong? What did you do and why should you call the attorney? And that's what I did. It took a little bit of adjustment, but once you get in front of the camera and you talk, you get comfortable and it's effective. And it's a much better way to do it than reading from an outline. That's what I learned today.

Honestly, I was a little nervous in the beginning about saying the wrong thing. One of the things that Gerry does to make you more comfortable is "Listen, you don't have to go from start to finish. We'll stop, we'll cut, but you have to be able to speak like you're talking to anybody else. Don't be formal. Don't act like a lawyer. Talk to them like you would talk to anybody."

In the beginning, that was nerve-racking but the more you do it, the more you get comfortable doing it, you just have to keep doing it, that's how you get better at it. I feel much more comfortable than I was this morning. I think I still have some more work to do, but the only way you're going to get better is you just keep doing it. That's it.

I think you did a great job and you had your work cut out for you, too. I think you did an excellent job."

Scott Harford, Esq.
Lynch Daskal Emery
264 West 40th Street
New York NY 10018
Phone: (212) 302-2400

How Not to Create Attorney Video

Often times it is just as important to know what not to do as it is to know what to do. As a trial attorney, I make every effort to go to every courtroom when I am in court. Not only do I enjoy watching other attorneys on trial, but I learn so much from other lawyers about what not to do. The same is true for video marketing. This is not your ordinary guide on how to create video. It's not a "best-practices" guide either. Instead, if you read this, it will show you how *not* to create video. It will help you from making the awful mistakes I see so often from attorneys and ordinary video companies. So, without further delay, let's get right to it.

1. SKIP YOUR CREDENTIALS

You should know by now that nobody cares where you went to school. Nobody. I am going to make you realize that all that money you spent on that really good law school doesn't make any difference when marketing your law firm online. Why not? Your consumer doesn't care. They don't want to know if you were on law review or moot court. It doesn't help solve their legal problem.

The only thing your potential client wants to know is if you have experience with their legal dilemma and can solve their problem. That's it. Do not even mention your credentials. Not needed. Not necessary.

Why not?

If you're giving useful information in a video, your consumer assumes that you are an attorney. They assume that you have experience. They assume that you know what you're talking about. If you talk to them about things they do not need or care about, they will look elsewhere.

2. NO NOSTRILS

If you use a laptop or webcam, you run the risk of having the camera look up at you. That creates two big problems. First is that you're looking down at your viewer; a psychological no-no. Second, they're looking up into your nostrils; also a big no-no. Nobody, and I mean nobody, wants to see what's inside your nostrils.

Think this doesn't happen? You're wrong. I've seen it and critiqued it at TechnoLawyer.com in my monthly video critique called YouLaw, also known as SmallLaw.

Be very careful where you place your camera. Keep it level with your face or slightly higher than you are. If you are looking down at your viewer, you will give the wrong impression. You will come across as high and mighty. You will appear condescending, regardless of how nice you are.

3. SPEAK CLEARLY

If you want your viewers to get to know you, they better be able to understand your words. If you don't speak clearly, your viewers will not stick around long to find out if they have a computer problem or their Internet connection is slow or you are just mumbling away.

I have watched many attorney videos where the lawyer mumbles their way through their message. I don't know what they were thinking, but they clearly did not have a viewer in mind and definitely did not watch their video prior to putting it online.

4. NO DISTRACTING BACKGROUNDS

That nice painting or sculpture you spent a fortune on is usually not the best background for your attorney video. It's often distracting and does nothing to enhance your message. Either find a neutral location to shoot your video or find things that are not offensive. Remember, not everyone has your taste in art.

Make sure that your plant or painting does not appear to be sticking out of your head, making you look really weird. I have seen it. There was one video in particular where the attorney was sitting in front of a painting of a large bull with massive horns. He had positioned himself directly in front of the bull's face. When the video was played, it looked as if the attorney had large horns coming out of both sides of his head. Funny? Yes. Wise move? Definitely not. He lost all credibility. If I couldn't take him seriously (and he was trying to be serious), then how could a consumer looking for his legal services?

5. NO NOISY LOCATIONS

Why do some lawyers feel the need to shoot crappy video in Starbucks or a noisy café? Do they think it adds panache and gravitas? The lawyers who create video in a noisy place think their microphone will eliminate all the ambient noise. They're wrong. Find a nice quiet place to shoot your video. It makes all the difference.

6. YOU'RE NOT DR. PHIL OR OPRAH

Some lawyers think it's fun to do a talk show, like Oprah. They think someone will watch a lawyer talking for 15–20 minutes about a topic they care little about or have no need for. Wrong.

Want to know why that type of show is not ideal? Simple. Lawyers are boring. Yes, it's true. The stuff we have to talk about is downright boring. Nobody cares what Rule 32 says. Nobody wants to know how an appellate court decided a particular issue… unless of course it relates directly to them.

7. NO BRIGHT WINDOWS

There are many lawyers who love to shoot video in front of the big picture window in their office. The video shoot goes well until they play the video back. Then they can't figure out why their window looks so bright and their face looks so dark. They haven't figured out the manual settings on their camera to adjust the lens exposure and correct it with additional lights.

It has to do with white balance and lens exposure. Stop shooting video in front of your window. Instead, close the shades and use light to illuminate.

8. NO WEBCAM

Does the word "pixelated" mean anything to you? It should. That's how most webcams create video. Pixelated. Jagged. Poor quality. Even with high-definition webcams, the glass (or plastic) is so small that the quality of the video is lacking. Webcams also do not have great color, and generally do poorly in low light.

9. NO FLIP CAMERA

When the Flip camera came on the market, it was the new, shiny toy. Then came the high-def version. The only problem with the original cameras was that there was only an onboard, built-in microphone and it picked up all ambient sound. Instead of fixing the problem, Kodak Zi8 beat Flip to the punch by creating a handy pocket camera in high-def with a wireless mic input.

Problem: There's no way to see yourself while shooting video, so it's difficult to know if you're properly in the camera frame. Also, indoor settings and quality are not nearly as good as a midrange, full-featured video camera.

Most video from the original Flip was terrible because of all the ambient sound from the built-in mic. For an on-the-spot, quick video this was fine. For creating an entire series of professional, quality-looking videos, it's not. Bottom line: You get what you pay for.

10. NO WIRED MIC

Want to trip over your wires while shooting video? Go ahead. Not a good idea. Want to know why the pros mostly use wireless mics? So the talent can walk around without a problem on the set and not trip over themselves.

11. NO SCRIPT

This is important. Any time a video producer tells you to use a script, I strongly suggest running the other way. Why?

When your prospective client is in your office and asks you a question, do you put your hand out to stop them and say, "Hold on… I have to run to my file cabinet to get the answer to your question"?

When you're standing in front of a jury during summations, do you think a jury will think highly of you and your client if you stand there reading a script? Not a chance.

Skip the script and use only outlines.

12. DO NOT UPLOAD DIRECTLY TO YOUTUBE

Why do lawyers still try to shoot a video on their iPhone and directly upload it to YouTube? Is the thinking, "I'd rather get something up right away," instead of "I'd rather produce a great quality video that's properly edited and create an image that my prospects want to see"?

Sometimes that's fine. Breaking news—good. New case law that your highest court just decided—good. On the street interview—good. Detailed explanation about a law-related topic—not good. Giving important information that explains to your client how and why something works—not good.

Also, YouTube is not the only place to upload your video. You must host your videos privately. You should also be uploading your videos to multiple video-sharing sites. Do not rely on one free video-sharing site to keep your videos forever or rely on it as the *only* source of traffic. Remember to diversify.

13. DO NOT USE TWITTER TO SAY, "CHECK IT OUT, MY NEW VIDEO"

Some automated services send out messages to your lists like Facebook and other social networks anytime you upload a video to YouTube or Facebook. Commonly the tweet reads "Check it out. New video about…"

That phrase, "Check it out," will virtually guarantee that your video will not be watched.

Why should I "check it out"? Your pithy message fails to answer that crucial question. If you are directing someone to do something, you better have a good reason and explanation to do so. Every time I see that phrase, I know that the attorney and his production company do not understand how to use social media to take advantage of spreading the word about their new video. Make sure you give your viewer a reason to watch.

14. DO NOT USE YOUR HAND TO HOLD YOUR CAMERA

Why do some lawyers continue to hold their video camera in their hand while shooting video? Do they really think they have a rock-solid ability to hold the camera still? Even the most steady hand has shake in it. Especially when holding a camera for a few minutes. This is true for many light, small, hand-held cameras.

The better practice is to use a tripod. That's the gold standard, and you can never go wrong using a tripod. "Steady as she goes" is a nautical phrase, but applicable to using a tripod to shoot your video on land.

15. NO LAPTOP

I have seen lawyers sitting in a noisy coffee bar, café, or restaurant shoot video using their laptops. They used the built-in iSight camera on their Mac, or the webcam attached to their laptop, along with the computer's built-in microphone. "Oy!"

is an expression that repeatedly comes to mind. "You must be kidding me," is a phrase my nine-year-old would use.

"Really? A webcam and built-in mic in a noisy setting? Really?" is what my 13-year-old daughter says.

If you want to use it to Skype with your friends or relatives, it's a great way to communicate instantly. But don't use it to create your important messages. Your prospects expect you to have some level of professionalism, regardless of what type of law you handle.

Besides, nobody can hear you well using your built-in microphone.

16. NO LEGAL ADVICE

That should be a no-brainer, right? Good.

Why then are some lawyers intent on giving legal advice online? Just because you put video online does not mean you can ever ignore your state's ethical rules. You must always adhere to the ethical guidelines governing lawyer advertising in your state. The fact that you are doing this online instead of offline is of no significance. Stay within your ethical boundaries at all times.

You know that information you put in a video may be timely and accurate today; however, it may be outdated and irrelevant a few days, weeks, months, or years from now. Your viewer may rely on that information to guide them regarding their legal options. If the information they've relied on is inaccurate, be prepared to send your malpractice carrier that dreaded letter letting them know you've just been served with a summons and complaint.

17. DO NOT AIM TO IMPRESS YOUR FRIENDS AND RELATIVES

If your goal is to impress your friends and colleagues with your ability to stand in front of a camera and talk, you are shooting video for the wrong reason. I have seen lawyers create video to show off how great they are, how wonderful they think they are, what great trial lawyers they are, and how they have really fancy offices.

That type of video may be right for the prospect who is only concerned about image. However, it's not going to cut it for the majority of your prospective clients. Someone searching for an attorney online wants information. They don't care whether your office has French chairs, Persian rugs, or hand-crafted moldings. They want your expertise and advice. The trappings of your office may be interesting to you, but offer no practical incentive to make you the attorney of choice over your competitor.

CONCLUSION

This list is by no means a complete list. Just spend a few minutes scouring attorney videos online and you'll see a host of good, bad, and ugly videos by attorneys seeking new business.

By following this list, you will have received useful information that will give you an edge over your competitors trying to do the same thing.

Did you also know that the Lawyers' Video Studio is the only place where an experienced medical malpractice trial attorney is also your video producer? It's the place where creating video is simple, easy, and fun. It's also the only place that allows you to create an entire video library of 50 videos in a one-day video shoot.

It's a place where you will learn about video content that increases the chances a viewer will convert to a caller. Remember, your video producer is the key to helping you develop content that your potential clients need and want to know. If your producer does not have a deep understanding of the practice of law and your ideal clients, how then can they help you create content that those people need to know?

YOU BRING OUT THINGS THAT THE OTHER MARKETING COMPANIES DON'T UNDERSTAND

"You bring out things that the other marketing companies don't understand. Things that are important for me to say to people and things that are important for me not to say on videos.

The way this started out was I wanted to be able to shoot videos in California without having to come to the East coast all the time. So, I hired a local guy to try and help me and he was a good technician but it just was not working, I wasn't able to get the help that I wanted with it.

When I talked to you Gerry, you understood right away what I needed and I felt that I would be better if you directed me. So I flew to New York from California and it's just been great. It's actually been a lot of fun.

You took a lot of time with me. You're very patient. We worked all day, just punched through from 9:30 to almost 4 o'clock now. Produced a lot of videos. There were a couple things, really, that I should have not been saying so we reshot that video with that content out. I just think we have a super product now.

I'm glad I came Gerry. Thank you for your help. I flew in yesterday, my wife and I flew over, stopped in Chicago and jumped on another plane into LaGuardia. Drove over here last night, stayed in Great Neck at a nice place, and shot video all day. You bought us a nice lunch and we're going to blast out of here tonight. So it was just 2 days. We'll be back. Real easy."

John Burns, Esq.
Personal Injury Trial Attorney
29222 Rancho Viejo Road #212
San Juan Capistrano, CA
(949) 496-7000

SCAN WITH YOUR SMARTPHONE TO WATCH & LISTEN TO JOHN BURNS' VIDEO.

Even More Things You Should Never Do with Video

1. DO NOT USE A FILM STUDENT TO SHOOT YOUR VIDEO

A lot of attorneys think they can go to a local film school and hire somebody with some experience shooting video. The reality is that you can. You can also hire a teenager in high school to use a camcorder to shoot your video without a tripod.

Then again, you can hire someone off the street to shoot your video too. Tell them to simply hold the camera as steady as possible while you try and talk. Ask those people whether they know what content gets a viewer to call you. Ask them if they know what problems your viewers have that they need answers to. They won't be able to answer those questions to your satisfaction.

2. NO GRAD STUDENTS NEED APPLY

I have nothing against grad students or film students. They're great. I love that they're learning how to shoot film and video. But there's the rub. They're learning. They're not lawyers. They're not experienced video producers. They don't know who your ideal clients are. They don't know what the ethical rules are. They don't know what you can and cannot say. Importantly, they don't know what content your viewers need and want to know. Nor, I dare say, do they know what content will get a viewer to convert to a caller.

If you are looking for a cheap way to create video, then by all means hire that film student or grad student. You'll save a bundle… in the short run. In the long run, you will probably wonder why you're not getting those calls you thought you'd be getting by creating attorney video to market your law practice.

3. SKIP SKYPE AND FOCUS ON QUALITY

I love Skype. It's a great tool. When my wife and I go to St. Maarten in the Caribbean without our kids, it's the best way to stay in touch with them, as if we're right at home with them. Video chatting with the kids is so much better than the phone. They get to see where we are (with a quick video tour of our hotel room), and we get to see who's doing homework and who's behaving or not, and the communication is instantaneous (assuming there's a good Internet connection).

The problem with Skype is that it's a tool used primarily for people who already have established a relationship. Those people—friends and family—don't really mind the jagged-edged video quality, the low-bandwidth hotel wireless Internet connection, and the poor lighting. That's understandable because they know you and are either related to you or already trust you.

However, to generate trust and confidence in your abilities as an outstanding lawyer, you need much more than Skype can currently provide. You need to use quality equipment to show your ideal clients that you are a professional. People perceive that you may not be ideal for them if you cannot get your technique to match their expectations.

4. NO GREEN SCREEN

Lawyers who try to use green screen think they can create stunning visual effects like superimposing scenes, moving images, and photos behind them when talking. That's what green screen allows you to do... with an important caveat: that you do it well. The problem? Making green screen work well takes lots of practice and experience. It's easy to make green-screen video really badly. However, it takes a really good production team to create a great quality green-screen video.

5. DO NOT STAND IN FRONT OF A LEGAL BOOKCASE

So many lawyers and video production companies like to shoot video in front of a legal bookcase. They think it gives them a more "professional" image. What they don't realize is that this type of image is boring and does nothing to show how the lawyer is different and stands out from the crowd.

Think about it. The fact that a lawyer stands in front of a bookcase is meaningless. What most consumers don't even realize is that most lawyers today don't even use the books on the shelves. Instead, everything is online and digital. We use our computers to do legal searches now. Why do some video companies continue to use that type of background image? Because they don't know any better.

6. NO MOOD LIGHTING

Here's what I mean. Some lawyers who try to shoot video on their own use the trial-and-error method of creating video. They try to create video using what they have, thinking they can cut corners. Most often, this results in dark and poorly illuminated video. This simply will not work.

Why do some lawyers think the fluorescent lights in their office are sufficient to illuminate them? I just don't get it. When you create video, you must *light up* your face. Not with spotlights, but with soft lights.

Some online gurus teach people how to create video for $20 by using homemade parts and existing lighting in their house.

While you certainly can be creative and use things that you already have, you must always keep in mind what the ultimate result will be and what result you want to achieve.

You have to understand your client's perceptions and what type of client you want to attract with the video message you are creating. If your ideal client is a 20-something who hangs out at Starbucks, then the webcam method with no additional lighting and no extra microphone may be the way to go. If, however, your client expects you to have a professional image, then you had better make sure that your video quality is up to their expectations.

You cannot skimp on lighting or audio. If either one of those elements are poorly done, your video will simply not be watched. The bar is set so high now that there is absolutely no excuse for you to have poor quality audio or video. Don't lose your potential clients because you decided to save a few dollars and go with your homemade lighting.

7. DO NOT LET YOUR VIDEO COMPANY ADVERTISE ON YOUR VIDEO

I cannot believe this is still done today. Video production companies like to advertise. They will often put their name on the intro graphic and the exit graphic of your video. In the early days of video production, they would also put the name of their video company on a graphic that stayed visible throughout the entire video. In addition, they will put their name and contact information in the description box of your video.

If that happens, ask yourself why you would allow a video company to advertise their services on your video? Are they paying you to advertise their services? Why should you allow them to post their contact information on your video?

The purpose of creating video is to communicate and educate your online viewers. By putting your video company's message on your video, the only thing you are telling your viewers is that this video company is advertising on your dime.

Do not let this happen to you. An established video production company does not need to plaster their name on your video. While it is nice to have people recognize what you do, it is simply not fair to the attorney or law firm since it dilutes the message, and it clearly shows this is a marketing or advertising piece.

By removing the video company's advertising message, your video message now becomes solely an educational message, which is exactly what you want to achieve.

8. DO NOT TALK ABOUT YOURSELF

"Come to me because I'm great! Come to me because I graduated at the top of my class! Come to me because of all my incredible credentials, and by the way, since you are here, let me list them all for you!"

For many years I have been telling lawyers to stop talking about themselves. Most listen; some do not.

There is a running debate online about which is the most important page of an attorney's website. Some legal marketing gurus believe an attorney's video bio is the most important component of their website. I totally disagree.

I think it is a waste of your resources and time to create a video bio. The reason? Because your online viewers simply don't care. Instead, they make a number of assumptions. An online viewer assumes you went to law school and successfully passed the bar. They assume you are licensed to practice law in your state and that you have some level of experience handling the type of cases you say you handle. Beyond that, your consumers really don't care about the awards you received in law school or what other law firms you worked for before arriving at your current destination.

Instead, they simply want to know how you can help solve their legal problem. Stop talking about yourself. Your viewer simply doesn't care.

9. DO NOT COMPARE YOURSELF TO ANYONE

You think you are better than most of the lawyers who compete with you. You know you're better than the guy who advertises on TV. You know you are a better attorney than the lawyers who advertise in the yellow pages. You know that those lawyers probably couldn't even find a courtroom if it was standing right in front of them. But then why are those attorneys getting all the good cases and you are not?

Lawyers are envious. Lawyers are competitive. They hate when their colleagues get better cases than they do. Some are tempted to point out in their marketing materials that they happen to be better lawyers than their competitors. While this seems like the right thing to do, I will tell you very clearly that it is not. Just like running a negative political campaign does very little to advance the politician's claims of how he can help his constituents, the same is true of lawyers who try and compare themselves to their competitors.

When comparing, some lawyers make the mistake of using their competitors' names. Doing so will open you up to a possible libel and/or slander suit. The better practice is never to mention your competitors by name. Rather than focusing on your competitors' weak points, simply eliminate that from your mind and focus instead on your strong points.

10. DO NOT BADMOUTH ANYONE

Anything you put online remains there forever. If you badmouth somebody during a rant in a blog post or a video, regardless of whether you remove it, that content is able to be found and remains online forever. Do not make the mistake of believing that by removing it a few days later it will not be found.

Many lawyers bitch and moan and complain about their biggest competitors. Some even throw accusations at their competitors about how they achieved certain results or obtained certain clients. If you badmouth another lawyer online by name, you will open yourself up to a grievance, as well as a possible libel and slander lawsuit. Those are things you simply do not want to get into since they are easily preventable.

Under no circumstance should you ever badmouth anyone in a video. Yet I see this happening on occasion and it bears mentioning. One of the cardinal rules of marketing yourself with video is never to badmouth your colleagues, competitors, or anyone for that matter.

Use video to educate your consumers and potential clients. Doing that is more effective than anything else you can do online.

WARNING: DON'T CREATE YOUR OWN ATTORNEY VIDEO TILL YOU READ THIS

Here's a perfect example of what happens when you think you can do it all yourself. A good friend of mine is a very sharp businessman. He wanted to create his own video to market his business. Great idea. The problem was the details.

I recently got an email from him, letting me know that the video file size was 39 GB large and was taking three days to upload to YouTube. He asked if this was normal.

I told him very clearly that his settings were all wrong. That file size is astronomically huge. Giganto. Humongo. Enormo. (How do you like those made-up words?)

I then recommended a few different ways to solve his problem. There are two great pieces of software that compress video to manageable sizes. However, unless you are willing to learn all about compression rate, frame rate, bit rate, audio compression, high-definition dimensions versus standard-definition dimensions, your video will not come out crystal clear in a size that is acceptable.

The other example I want to share with you is an attorney who told me how he wanted to do his videos. He said he was very comfortable with the TV ads he created and wanted to use the same theme and slogans as in his TV ads. I was polite but very firm. "No. That's not what online video is about. It's totally different than TV ads. The people who are watching TV ads have a totally different mindset than viewers who are online searching for an attorney."

If you want to create video on your own, keep in mind that the devil is in the details. Also, the content you may be really familiar with will not work as online video. You need to create content your viewers need and want to know. You want to practice law and leave the marketing to someone else. That's where we come in. We do that. In fact, I do all three:

1. I am a practicing New York medical malpractice lawyer.

2. I created a done-for-you service to create 50 videos in a one-day video shoot.

3.   I show you a viewer's mindset and how to create content your viewers want and need to know.

CONCLUSION

Video is the most effective way to communicate with your online consumers and potential clients. It is the most cost-effective way to do that and the most highly targeted tool you can use today that will help online consumers who are looking for an attorney.

Consumers expect you to have video. Take the time to do it right and your video investment will pay off for years to come. Do it wrong and you'll have wasted your time, energy, and resources.

I encourage you to call me for a free marketing strategy session to see if I can help you market your law firm using online video. It'll be the best marketing time you spend all year. You can set up your call by contacting my production manager, Kathleen, at 800-320-4314 or by email: Kathleen@ LawyersVideoStudio.com. I welcome your call.

GERRY IS AN ABSOLUTE MASTER AT GETTING YOU TO RELAX AND SPEAK TO THE CAMERA

"Hi. This is DJ Banovitz. I'm a personal injury lawyer in Denver, Colorado and I've just completed my video shoot with Gerry Oginski. Well, prior to coming in today, there was a mastermind session with Gerry where we discussed what my topics would be and how best to prepare myself for the video shoot today.

So, as a result of that, I came in with a very good idea with all the topics I was going to discuss on the videos and how to go about doing that in the most effective manner with potential clients. I have never done any sort of videos before and came in somewhat nervous and Gerry is an absolute master at getting you to relax and speak to the camera in such a way that the clients, the potential client, are going to be receptive to the message that you're giving them.

I decided to use video to market my law firm because YouTube is the second largest video search website on the Internet, next to Google. At some point in time, it is probably going to overtake Google. So, I think it's absolutely critical to have content out there to appeal to potential clients in your practice area.

I chose Gerry to help me because I had been thinking about shooting video for a long time and had researched doing it on my own, planning the learning curve on my own, hiring video studios where you got to their video studio and you shoot a handful of videos and you're done.

What I've found is that the learning curve to do it by yourself and learn all the editing and everything else is simply too steep, and I wanted to focus on what I do best which is practicing law. And likewise, by going to one of these video studios it's a one-time deal where you shoot a handful of videos, it's expensive, and you're done and over with.

Gerry is the only one who offers a Total Video Solution where not only do you shoot a significant number of videos, but you're provided with the equipment so that you can continue to shoot videos and stay ahead of your competition in your marketplace.

The process is that I had outlined several topics that I wished to discuss and I would do a little bit of practice with Gerry, and we would do however many takes was required to have the video come off as smoothly as possible. Gerry was absolutely spot on with his suggestions in how to make the videos interesting and to appeal to potential clients.

One of the principal reasons I selected Gerry to help me with my videos is that Gerry is an acting, practicing trial lawyer and nobody else knows what an acting, practicing trial lawyer is faced with on a day to day basis.

I have absolutely no doubt in my mind that a video producer or production company that is inexperienced in the ins and outs of personal injury law, would have anywhere near the ability to effectively coach and shoot content as Gerry has.

If somebody came to me and asked me "DJ, do you think it's a good idea to shoot video and who would you have shoot video for you?" I would encourage them to first think about doing it on their own. Then, seek out and search video studios that can do it, and then after you've learned a lot, I would go to Gerry Oginski and really learn what a master in this area can do for you. It is absolutely clear that Gerry's understanding of shooting video, in particular for personal injury trial lawyers, is so far beyond anybody else in this area that you would doing yourself a real disservice if you spent your money any other way."

DJ Banovitz, Esq.
Personal Injury Trial Lawyer
7887 East Belleview Avenue #1100
Englewood, CO 80111
(303) 300-5060

SCAN WITH YOUR SMARTPHONE TO WATCH & LISTEN TO DJ BANOVITZ'S VIDEO.

Two Things Never to Talk About on Video

You would think that this is self-explanatory by now. Unfortunately, it's not. Years ago the production companies would tell lawyers that their potential clients wanted to hear all about their credentials and how great they were. Who were we, as lawyers, to disagree?

1. DON'T TALK ABOUT YOURSELF

What great knowledge and insight did we have, as mere practicing attorneys, to dispute what these wise production companies had to say? That's why most video marketing was terrible when it first became popular on the web about five or six years ago. Most video production companies still had the yellow pages mentality, thinking that if the lawyer talked about his or her credentials and all of their great experience, that would be an incentive to get someone to call.

It makes sense in a weird sort of way. However, as more and more people went online to search for information, it became apparent that the old-school style of creating marketing messages had changed. It changed so dramatically that viewers no longer cared about what law school you went to and what your qualifications were. The mind shift occurred because they realized they could bypass the TV ads and the yellow pages and find direct content about their particular legal problem.

There was a huge disconnect between what people were searching for and what lawyers and their video production companies were providing to them. The savvy lawyers who were learning to market their practices by learning from others outside the legal community, recognized quickly that potential clients did not care about us as individuals. Rather, the only thing they cared about was whether we could help solve their pressing legal problem. If we could somehow show that we had the knowledge and intelligence to solve their problem, that enabled us to dramatically increase the chances that they would recognize us as an expert, without ever having to say that we were, in fact, an expert.

Useful Information Is More Interesting than Your Bio

There are still some lawyers and video companies who believe that it is important to have the lawyers talk about themselves. I've stated repeatedly, lecturing to attorneys throughout the country as well as writing hundreds of articles about video marketing for lawyers, that your consumer and potential client who is searching for you online simply does not care about you. Assuming that fact to be true, why then would you create a video that talks about you?

I have had smart lawyers tell me that they wanted to create an attorney bio in a video to supplement their bio page on their website. I told them that would be a waste of their time and resources, precisely because people are not coming to the bio page until they have already determined that they like what you have to say and have begun to trust you, based upon the information you have already provided to them.

You gain much more traction by providing useful content than you do by talking about yourself or your law firm. Think about it this way: When you go to buy a new car, do you really care whether the car dealer has sold 10 cars that month or 100 cars? Do you really care how long the car dealer has been in business in order for them to sell you a car that you want? The reality is that you don't care a bit about any of the salesman's credentials. You only want information about the car that will help you to make a purchasing decision.

2. DON'T TALK ABOUT THE LAW

Again, this should be common sense that you should never talk about the law in your videos, because you do not want to establish an attorney-client relationship with someone who's watching your video online. You also do not want someone to incorrectly apply the information you are discussing, since they may inaccurately interpret what you are saying. In addition, you may be providing information that may be out of date the following day, week, month, or year. By the time a viewer watches your information, they may not recognize that the information is untimely or has changed.

Under no circumstance should you provide legal information without providing a huge disclaimer both verbally and in written form. In fact, if a lawyer in my Lawyers' Video Studio program is going to discuss a specific law, I make sure that they include a verbal disclaimer that the viewer cannot and should not be relying on this information.

That is a responsible way to present information to the general public. It also will conform with your state's ethics rules.

Ethics Rules Apply to Video

Lawyers must keep in mind that all of their attorney videos must comply with the ethical rules specific to your own state. If there is something that you cannot do online or off-line, take that to heart, and under no circumstance should you create a video that risks stepping over the boundaries of what the ethics committee believes is appropriate.

I recently critiqued a video by an attorney who created a video as if he were talking to the jury. He disclosed "secrets" about things that a jury should not know during the course of the trial. Specifically, he disclosed that there *is* available insurance coverage in personal injury and medical malpractice cases. That is certainly the case here in New York. However, this lawyer was confiding and disclosing these "secrets" to these jurors as if they were in the middle of watching the trial.

In fact, the attorney specifically said that jurors are not supposed to know this information, and that he is not supposed to disclose this. If true, then why would he be creating a video that informs the general public about something he knows that he cannot disclose or discuss in front of a jury? I do believe he has opened a can of worms for himself, simply because he knows this topic is off-limits yet has chosen to reveal this information to the general public.

Although the video was done as an educational video, he cannot ignore his state's own ethics rules. Make sure you abide by your ethical rules. Lawyers who participate in my video program are told at the outset that under no circumstance will they be creating any video that is in a gray area. It must be either black or white. This way, no attorney will ever have to worry about saying something that exceeds the boundaries of what is appropriate for online video marketing.

ULTIMATELY I USED GERRY BECAUSE HE IS A PRACTICING ATTORNEY...

"Hello. I'm attorney Charles Pitman in Huntsville, Alabama, a personal injury lawyer. And I've been working with Gerry Oginski at the Lawyers Video Studio and I'd like to say a few words about that now.

You know, about the process throughout the day I didn't know what to expect entirely. I expected to come in and be able to sit down and read through the videos, talk through the videos, and move very quickly. I think that preparation is key. Preparation is very important because it allows the day to flow smoother, allows you to get a lot more videos, it just makes the day progress more smoothly.

I decided to create a whole video library to help educate consumers in my market about auto accidents and other injury claims, and also to help supplement other advertising that I'm doing with some online video and website advertising.

I chose not to do this on my own because I do not have the time to sit down and put all this together and figure it all out. And I wanted sort of a turnkey solution. Someone who could come in, help me get it done, just like this in a day, and not take six months to figure it out myself.

Well, Gerry definitely understands what the legal terms are. He's familiar with the law so it makes today go a lot smoother. Instead of having a non-legal non-lawyer coach who doesn't really know what they're talking about, Gerry is in the trenches and understands it. He knows how to speed the process along and how to keep you on track and on target.

I decided to go with Gerry because he offered his services for free...I'm just kidding. I was actually looking at using Lawyers Video Studio and this other website company that shot video.

Ultimately I used Gerry because he is a practicing attorney and I wanted to be able to do this on my own and have my own equipment, learn how to do this. I didn't want to be tied having to go to a specific location and travel every time I wanted to shoot videos and incur that repetitive travel costs. I wanted someone to come help me and get me set up and give me an option of doing it on my own, with some supplemental help through the process.

I definitely recommend Gerry. I think it's a great program and I have been here all day and I've shot, I don't know, 40, 50 videos. [Gerry's note: Charles shot 75 videos in one day!] It's hard to get that done if you're doing it on your own or you have to go to a studio somewhere. I would definitely recommend this to any colleague or friend."

Charles Pitman, Esq.
Charles Pitman Injury Lawyers, LLC
8075 Madison Boulevard, Suite 112
Madison, Alabama 35758
(256) 533-5000

**SCAN WITH YOUR
SMARTPHONE** TO WATCH
& LISTEN TO CHARLES
PITMAN'S VIDEO.

You Can Do This Too

Creating video to market your law firm is one of the more creative ways to express yourself. It is one of the more interesting ways to use your knowledge and expertise to help others.

Grabbing a video camera and pressing the record button is the simplest thing you can do. However, before rushing out to start shooting your own video, keep in mind that the majority of attorney video online today is crap—from a technical standpoint and from a content standpoint.

There are a lot of really smart attorneys out there who believe that they can create great quality video that will capture the minds and hearts of their viewers. The problem is that many of them don't understand the necessary and basic techniques to create good quality video. They also fail to understand the psychology that drives the viewer to pick up the phone and call.

Admittedly, lawyer video hasn't improved dramatically over the past few years. Lawyers and video companies have gotten smarter with experience. Yet there are many video companies creating attorney video that still have the mindset of TV broadcast.

You can learn how to be a great videographer, a super video editor, and a terrific video publisher. Information is available for you to become an expert in each of these categories. For those lawyers who have the desire and inclination to be all those things in addition to a practicing attorney, congratulations! However, the majority of lawyers today have no interest or desire to learn a new trade in order to market themselves or their law firm. Rather, they would prefer to hire an experienced video marketing company to do this for them.

In this chapter I'm going to lay out the basics to get you started.

IDEAS

The very first thing you must do in order to create great video is to sit down at the table with pen and paper and start coming up with great ideas. This has nothing to do with equipment yet. It has nothing to do with the location where you shoot your video. It has nothing to do with the clothes you will wear on the day of your video shoot. Rather, this is all about mindset and what information your client needs to know, not information that you want to tell them.

I will tell you that coming up with ideas will seem difficult at first. That's only because you haven't tried it before. Once you understand what type of information you need to provide, then you will immediately have that "aha" moment where every time you look around you'll get another idea.

I could be standing at the checkout line in the grocery store and come up with five new ideas for video topics. I could be waiting in the car, picking up my daughter from middle school, and come up with new ideas for video topics. I could be in the middle of a phone consultation with a potential new client and come up with three new ideas for video. The information is right in front of your eyes; you just don't realize it yet.

A WORD OF WARNING

Do not copy your competitors' content. We as lawyers believe that our competitors are doing well with their marketing and have always thought of a copycat approach to marketing. Here's why you do not want to copy your competitors' content:

1. It's wrong on so many levels.

2. You have no idea whether the content they have created is generating calls to their office.

3. Copying someone else's content means that you are not creative enough to come up with your own ideas.

This means that you will have no way to distinguish yourself from your competitor.

4. Your goal when creating video is to stand out from the crowd. If you try and copy your colleagues' content, then there is no way for a viewer to distinguish you from them.

5. If you do not understand the motivating psychology behind the video, then it will be unlikely that you will achieve any real success creating a similar video.

Okay, so you are willing to get started on the road to creating video on your own. Let's get right to it.

The easiest way to start is to create a list of the 10 most frequently asked questions that people ask when they come into your office. The answers to those questions will provide you with the substance necessary to fill those initial videos.

My best-practices recommendation is to provide only one question and one answer per video. The reason? Viewers who are searching for information will turn away if you have multiple questions and multiple answers in one video. Your viewer wants specific information. If you go off topic beyond what they are searching for, you will lose them. Remember, one question and one answer per video.

CHOOSING YOUR EQUIPMENT

You need a video camera, microphone, and lights. There are hundreds and hundreds of possible combinations of equipment that you can purchase. In fact, the selections are overwhelming.

The choice of equipment that you purchase depends entirely on your budget, what you can afford, and the quality of video you want to create.

When deciding what type of equipment to buy, keep in mind two things: (1) Your viewer somehow believes that your legal ability correlates with your video quality. (2) Do not buy equipment with all the bells and whistles when you are just starting out, believing that you will grow into it as a budding videographer. The better practice is to buy equipment at the basic level, learn how to use all of its functions well, and as you get better, then you can upgrade your equipment at a later time.

Here are some caveats though.

Camera

Do not use your laptop, webcam, flip cam, or bloggie to create video. These can all create high-definition video, but the better practice is to use a moderately priced video camera to get your content online.

I use three different cameras for different situations, and I will briefly explain what I use later.

If you are looking for recommendations, then you can start out looking at the Canon Vixia line of video cameras. They take great quality video and are priced to fit every budget.

Microphone

Next, you need a microphone to attach to your camera. Never rely on the built-in microphone, since that will pick up the noise from the video camera itself together with all the ambient noise in the room. You can buy a wired microphone or a wireless microphone. You can buy a shotgun microphone that sits on top of your camera and looks like a long probe with a windscreen.

For great quality audio, I highly recommend a wireless lapel microphone. This will allow you the freedom to walk around without worrying about tripping over wires. If you are less inclined to buy a wireless microphone set including a transmitter and receiver, then I recommend the Rode shotgun video microphone that currently costs about $150 at B&H Photo or on Amazon.

If you plan on creating video for a number of years, then I highly recommend getting the best quality audio equipment you can afford. Having crystal-clear audio is an extremely important component of creating great quality video.

Alternatively, you can go into RadioShack and buy a $10 wired microphone that will get you audio. It will be a slight improvement over your built-in microphone. However, in terms of audio quality, you will quickly learn why the $10 wired microphone costs $10 as opposed to a $600 microphone. The quality is remarkably different.

When I first started creating video, I didn't know the difference and made the mistake of starting out with a cheap microphone. I did not understand why the audio sounded like I was in a tin can. I didn't know any better. There was no one around that I could ask for advice or assistance to explain what type of audio equipment I should buy to achieve good audio.

I personally use a wireless lapel microphone that cost $600. It is an extremely consistent and reliable system and has been worth every penny to me. However, starting out, I clearly did not have the budget to buy a $600 microphone, nor did I have any idea how to best use such a microphone.

You can buy a wireless microphone from $150 up to $3,000. Again, it all depends on your budget and your technical ability. A good friend of mine recently asked me what microphone I would recommend to do a two-person sitdown interview. I gave him a few different options. The first two options were extremely technical and involved multiple wireless microphones, transmitters, and receivers, together with adapters that would allow him to get great quality audio for both the person being interviewed and the person conducting the interview.

The problem was that this was way too technical for anyone trying to do something simple. The obvious option was a shotgun microphone that sits on top of his video camera.

Lights

You must have supplemental lights when shooting video. Do not rely on whatever lights are in your office or home. Your video will come out dark, and you will not understand why you look dark. Again, your choices are wide and varied. You can get halogen lights, fluorescent lights, LED lights, and more. You can go with homemade lights, work lights, and even candles.

My best-practices recommendation is to stay away from the homemade lights, candles, flashlights, lamps, and halogen lights. The easiest and least costly investment to illuminate you on video is fluorescent lights in the form of soft boxes. A soft box is a device that provides diffuse light at a consistent temperature. With fluorescent lighting you never have to worry about burning your hands, since they are generally much cooler to the touch than halogen lights.

You need at least two soft-box lights. I personally use four or five lights when I shoot video; however, there are many times where I only use two. There are many companies selling lights that cost from $100 to $5,000, depending upon the type and quality of lights you want. There are different wattages and color temperatures and control settings for each of the lights. Every light you buy will have a tripod to attach it to. Most soft-box lights will come with two to six fluorescent lights, and many will have control switches allowing you to control or dim the amount of light it puts out. The soft box looks like something has been draped over your lights.

USING YOUR EQUIPMENT

When first starting out, you will need to learn the basics of each piece of your equipment and how to apply that knowledge to setting up your scene before you ever press the record button.

Here are some of the basics with each piece of equipment you use.

Camera

Always shoot in high definition. That is the standard online today. Always use the highest quality settings on your camera, because when you take the video off the camera and put it onto the computer, it will need to be processed and compressed. By the time you get that video online, it will have been compressed multiple times. If you do not use the highest quality settings, you will wind up with video quality settings that are not ideal.

You will need to understand what frame rate to shoot your video at. You can shoot at 24 frames per second, 25 frames per second, 29 frames per second, 30 frames per second, or 60 frames per second, and then you must decide whether to use interlaced or progressive video area. Most video cameras in the United States will shoot at 30 frames per second. If you're buying a camera today or have bought one recently, in all likelihood you will be using a camera that has an internal hard drive or records to a memory card. Tape drives are old school. If you are recording to a memory card, you need to get at least a class 6 memory card, which is a high-capacity, high-density, and high-speed memory card that will allow you to record at the highest settings.

Microphone

If you are using a wireless microphone, you must become familiar with and develop an expertise with setting the proper audio levels and frequencies. Since this is a wireless device, it is subject to interference. Depending upon where you live and what other frequencies are being used, it is possible that you will get audio "hits" during your video shoot. That is why it is critical to replay the video immediately after doing a few test runs to listen for any audio interference. If you encounter interference or occasional audio hits, you will need to change the frequency so you have a clear audio channel. Your wireless microphone should have multiple audio frequencies to choose from in the event you notice audio interference.

Lights

You need to play with the lighting equipment and learn how to set it up and take it down so that it becomes second nature. You will need extension cords and power strips and additional bulbs. You will need to decide whether you will be leaving these lights in one location or taking them down after each video shoot.

When I shoot video in my office, I leave my lights off in the corner of my office and they make a great conversation starter anytime someone comes into the office. People always see my video equipment and start asking me questions about it. If you do not have the space or the desire to leave your equipment out, then you must learn how to disassemble it and pack it up. Setting up all this equipment for your first video shoot will be time-consuming and frustrating. Taking down the equipment and putting it away will appear to be much faster, but will still take significant time to pack up. As with anything else, the more you use it, the better and quicker you will become.

When I first started creating video, it would not be uncommon for me to take 45 minutes to set up my equipment. It would take me another half an hour to get the settings all correct and make sure I was properly framed. Now I can do that in 10–15 minutes. Taking down the equipment takes me about 10–15 minutes now.

YOUR CLIENTS DON'T CARE ABOUT YOUR EQUIPMENT

Your client doesn't care what camera you own. They don't give a hoot about your microphone. Nor do they care about whether your lights are at 5600 kelvin or daylight temperature.

"Well, if they don't care about me or my equipment, what the heck *do* they care about?"

I'm glad you asked. Here's what they care about:

1. Your message

2. Information that you can give them about *their* legal problem

3. Explanations that help them understand the predicament they're in

4. Partial explanations that *show* them you help people with the problems they have

5. That you have the answers and solutions to *their* problems

That's it.

They have a legal problem.

They don't know a lawyer.

They need a lawyer.

How are you different from your colleagues?

The equipment you use and your video technique should be totally transparent. Your viewer should *only* be paying attention to your message and not to whether you have a technically brilliant video.

The problem for most lawyers trying to shoot video on their own is that there's a huge learning curve to do it right and do it well. The bar has been set really high with high-definition video being the standard now.

SOMEONE WHO I TRUST, LEGAL MARKETING EXPERT HENRY HARLOW TOLD ME TO TALK TO YOU. HE SAID YOU WERE THE BEST.

"I'm Steve Kramer of the Kramer law firm. I'm a Florida attorney. I think video provides an interactive marketing solution that really lets you connect with your client before they ever talk to you and I'm a believer in Internet marketing. One of the problems with internet marketing is that there's a lot of concentration and focus on search engine optimization and search engine marketing. But, it doesn't matter how many people you get to your website if it doesn't convert to leads, if it doesn't convert to clients.

The way I view it is that video interaction is more likely to lead to a connection to a client and lessen the bounce rate, which is when people go to your website and then just bounce off.

Someone who I trust, legal marketing expert Henry Harlow told me to talk to you. He said you were the best.

I was pleased with the way you do videos, that's innovative. I like the method; I like the focus on the client rather than the attorney, because that fits with the model of my firm. I try to be a client-orientated firm rather than, I don't know, not client-orientated is the only other option. But I thought that fit with it. I thought that would speak and appeal to potential clients more than me speaking about myself which is really the paradigm that most of the marketing world for law works.

We probably created, I don't know, by the end of the day today hopefully we will have created about 90 videos. I feel like I have set a new bar and a new record. I challenge any of you to beat that record. Anybody who's trying to do 50 videos and wants good, quality work product I would recommend not waiting until the weekend before and start cramming for your video shoot.

Don't, for example, wait for a couple days before it and then assign the creation of outlines to your staff. Don't try to wing it and improvise and do that stuff, because that's not articulate.

Well, you know, right now it's impossible to say what the end result is going to be because you know I haven't put them in the marketplace. But as far as filming the videos, it's a good experience and I like the model and I think we did good work product today. I think that video is the future and you're looking 5 years down the road, I think that the importance of television and radio are going to diminish and the importance of Internet is going to rise.

I think that anybody seeking to get a competitive advantage in that market needs to take the initiative and work on that now. And this is an opportunity to get ahead of the curve and gain a competitive advantage that creates a connection with the client and that also gives you an advantage as far as the search engine optimization, as far as conversions, as far as lessening your bounce rate, as far as being a more effective marketing machine."

Steven Kramer, Esq.
Bankruptcy, Foreclosure & Family Law Attorney
The Kramer Law Firm
999 Douglas Avenue, Suite 3333
Altamonte Springs, FL 32714
877.493.4847

SCAN WITH YOUR SMARTPHONE TO WATCH & LISTEN TO STEVEN KRAMER'S VIDEO.

Don't Believe the Hype; Your Video Equipment Is Meaningless

A few years ago I wrote a blog post titled "It's Not the Size of Your Equipment that Matters."

That double entendre got a lot of laughs. However, most lawyers who want to create video get so hung up on what type of equipment to use that they forget about the forest for the trees. It's easy to get lost in the abundance of available video equipment since there are hundreds of variations of cameras on the market as well as microphone equipment and lighting equipment. Your choices are limited only by your budget and the quality of video that you want to create. Keep in mind, however, that your viewer believes that your legal ability is somehow correlated to your video ability.

I always get a good laugh when marketing gurus tell lawyers how easy it is to run out and buy the latest pocket camera with high-definition video, shoot a quick video (either hand-held at arm's length or on a tripod), and immediately upload it to YouTube.

IT'S NOT THE SIZE OR THE COST OF YOUR EQUIPMENT

You can use a $200 video camera to create great quality video that can compete with someone using a $3,000 camera. It's not the equipment that matters. You can buy a $100 wired microphone that will produce decent audio or you can buy a $600 wireless microphone that will produce great audio as long as there is no radio interference. You could easily spend $1,500 on a set of soft-box lights that produce nice, soft, even lighting or, on the other hand, you could use a couple of makeshift lights or even natural light to create a nice video.

Let me say it again. The size of your equipment and the type of your equipment does not really matter. *All things being equal (which they are not), it is the message that you are attempting to get online that will distinguish you from all of the lawyers who compete with you.*

Your goal is to create a technically proficient video that is transparent and seamless. What that means is that your video technique, your lighting technique, and your audio technique must be perfect (within reason) so that your viewer focuses solely on the message you are attempting to tell them, rather than being distracted by the imperfect video techniques you have used.

If creating video was really as easy as some marketing experts would lead you to believe, then there would be no videos online that I could use for educational teaching purposes when I lecture to attorneys across the country to show what not to do.

However, I hasten to say, there are an abundant number of really smart lawyers who create really bad video. They have the best intentions, yet fail to execute and implement properly. Even more astounding is that these lawyers fail to recognize that their masterpiece video creations do much more harm than good.

If you think you need the latest JVC high-end professional camera that costs $3,000 because it integrates beautifully with Final Cut Pro, I will tell you that it is a beautiful video camera. It is small, relatively light, and has every professional function you could ever imagine. However, you could just as easily buy a Canon Vixia camcorder for $500. For the purposes of putting video online, you get similar quality for a fraction of the cost. Remember, this is not broadcast quality TV. This is not an indie film being promoted at the Sundance Film Festival.

MY VIDEO EQUIPMENT

For years I loved using my Canon Vixia HF S10 camcorder to create video. It cost $1,200 when I bought it. This camera model is no longer made, and the top-of-the-line Canon Vixia will set you back almost $1,500. I also loved to use my Canon

T2i dSLR. I have recently outgrown my T2i and upgraded to a Canon 60D dSLR for both video and photography. The 60D will run you about $900, and lenses will cost anywhere between $400 and $1,000 depending on the type of lens you need.

The really cool thing about using my dSLR is that I'm able to get an incredible depth of field that you do not ordinarily see with a camcorder. Depth of field gives you the ability to keep yourself in focus and everything in your background blurred. That type of effect can be very powerful if you know how to use it well. It forces the viewer to pay attention to you, in perfect focus, while eliminating distractions in the background.

I also use a Sony NEX VG20 professional video camera with interchangeable lenses to shoot video. This camera will set you back about $2,300. This is best used as a camera where you set all functions manually to achieve best results.

For most lawyers who want to create quick video without learning how to be a professional photographer or videographer, I recommend using an automatic camcorder to do this. Skip the manual dSLR unless photography is your passion.

My recommendation to attorneys is that you should use whatever you have to start your videos. I still would stay away from your iPhone and the pocket cams and instead focus on a moderately priced camera, microphone, and lights. Once you become more proficient at creating video, then look to upgrade. Another alternative is to buy used equipment when you upgrade, which will save you considerable money.

FOCUS ON YOUR MESSAGE

Rather than focus on the equipment, focus on what you are trying to say to your consumer. Remember, if you cannot capture your viewer's attention within the first three to five seconds, it doesn't matter what your message is or what equipment you use to create your video. Your viewer is gone. If they found your video and clicked on it to watch it, you have to hold their attention for the first five seconds. Then you need some really good content that educates and informs them about something they didn't already know.

Remember my two rules of creating video:

1. Never talk about yourself.

2. Never talk about the law.

My first rule always applies since our viewers don't care about us. Instead they want to know how you can help solve their problems. My second rule also is a commandment since you do not want anyone relying on legal information you provide in the video.

Focus on the message and your viewer will quickly realize that you are the go-to expert for more information. Teach, educate, and become a resource. Start the conversation, and before you know it, people will be contacting you to ask you questions about their legal problems. That's how it works. That's why the size and type of your equipment just don't matter.

I TRULY APPRECIATE YOUR WELL-INFORMED COACHING TO HELP ME GET THROUGH THE PROCESS TODAY

"I'm Richard Habiger, an elder law attorney in Southern Illinois, specifically Carbondale in deep Southern Illinois. Gerry, I want to thank you a heck of a lot. I lost my PowerPoint. I had planned to use my laptop along with my PowerPoint to guide me as we created these videos, but thanks to you, you were able to coach and cajole me into creating what hopefully will be works of art.

Whether they are works of arts or not, I really truly appreciate your kind and gentle and well-informed coaching to help me get through the process today in creating the videos. Video is, in my opinion, the next thing to help market legal services on the Internet, on websites. My website is not doing what I anticipated. It's my hope that with videos, it will be a destination spot for social workers, financial professionals and other attorneys who are looking to make referrals to my office.

Whether it's a son or a daughter in New York, Florida, Texas, California, or someone who is in Southern Illinois who has perhaps haven't heard about us and finds us on the web. Hopefully, they will see our videos and perhaps one viewing will be enough, but perhaps they have siblings that they will want to also see the videos. They can direct them to the videos and as a family, pre-sell themselves in a manner of speaking.

I used to use an audio CD and when it first came out, when I first started using audio CDs, they were very helpful but it seemed like quite a few people were using audio CDs then. Frankly, there's nothing like a picture. A picture tells a thousand words and when it's a talking picture, hopefully ten thousand words.

Gerry, I want to tell you why I chose your services as opposed to somebody else's services.

First, even though I like to do stuff myself, you offer a total video package. You provided me with the equipment and the coaching and know how so that I'm able to produce additional videos on an ongoing basis over time. That's frankly what sold me so that I would not have to continue to come back here to New York or for you to trek to Southern Illinois to create videos. Instead, with your coaching, I'll create the videos, ship the memory card to you so that you get to work your magic. Hopefully, you'll make me sound like Clark Gable. Thank you very much again Gerry."

Richard Habiger, Esq.
Habiger & Associates Elder Law Office
2010 West Woodriver Drive
Suite 100
Carbondale, Illinois 62901
618-549-4529 or 800-336-4529

CHAPTER 17

210

Step-by-Step Video Guide

I recently created a "State of the Internet" address for attorney video and during my presentation explained why most attorney video stinks. To understand why, you need to recognize two components to create great quality video:

1. Mastering the video equipment and software

2. Figuring out what content will compel a viewer to pick up the phone and call you instead of your competitor

Some lawyers like to do things themselves and would rather spend their time to learn how to do a new task rather than pay someone to do it. That's okay. However, it's not always a good thing. If your roof leaks, do you go up and fix it or call a roofer? If your sink is clogged, do you fix it yourself or call a plumber? If your car breaks down, do you hoist it up on blocks in your driveway and work on it for two weeks, or do you have it towed to the local mechanic?

It is often better to leverage your time with someone else's expertise. What do I mean? Think about how valuable your time is. You could learn how to become a videographer, video editor, and video publisher to market your practice. If you elect to do that, prepare to spend hundreds and thousands of hours of your time perfecting those skills. Then ask yourself whether you can better devote that time and energy to your law practice and your family.

To give you an idea of what it takes to become an expert at all things video, I'm going to take you through, step-by-step, what you need to know to create great quality video.

Don't let anyone tell you that it's a simple matter of taking a Kodak Zi8 camera and pressing the red record button and then directly uploading to YouTube. I've seen too many awful lawyer videos created that way. That's not quality video.

As with anything in life, if you are going to take the time to learn to do something, take the time to learn to do it well. At the end of this chapter, ask yourself if this is what you really want to do.

Here's my step-by-step video guide.

GETTING SET UP

High-Definition Camera

Find the appropriate high-definition video camera to create your video. There are literally hundreds of choices on the market today, with prices ranging from $75 to $10,000. In the "old days" you had much fewer choices, and you only had to decide whether you wanted a tape-based or disk-based video camera. Do you want HD or SD? Memory card or flash?

My favorite camera on my wish list is a JVC video camera that costs nearly $3,000. The reason why it costs so much? Because it works seamlessly with Apple's Final Cut Pro and makes it as simple as dragging and dropping content from the camera directly onto the timeline, without having to transcode it before uploading and editing. Transcoding is when you take the video off your camera and put it on your computer. You can't simply drag it into your editing software if it's in a format your editor doesn't recognize. It has to be converted to the proper format before you can edit. That's transcoding.

Audio

Next, determine what type of audio you're going to use to create your video. After the video camera, audio equipment is typically the most expensive component of your video setup. If you do not have crystal-clear audio, I don't care what content you have, nobody will watch it.

You have a choice of using a wired microphone or a wireless microphone. The cost of microphones ranges from $10 to $5,000. You know the phrase "You get what you pay for"? I thought I knew better. When I started making video, I spent hours shooting with my new economical microphone. When I put the video on my computer, I finally learned my lesson. Aggravation and frustration were the keywords of the day.

Needless to say, those videos never made it online since the audio quality was terrible.

Wireless microphones are the microphones of choice. Again, you have a wide variety and quality. The benefit of using a wireless microphone is that you do not trip over the wires as you move around your office when you shoot video. The disadvantage is that sometimes other electronics may interfere with the frequency that you are transmitting on. Depending upon the quality of your wireless microphone, you may or may not have the ability to change frequencies to eliminate this problem.

After my audio debacle, I decided to invest in a professional wireless microphone system that cost me $600. It was the best investment I made.

Illumination

"Lights!" You have to learn what lights are ideal for your video. You have to understand why lighting is so crucial to illuminate you, the room you're in, and your background. If you do not illuminate properly, your videos will *not* be watched.

Once you recognize the absolute need for lights, you have many choices. Do you get halogen lights or fluorescent lights? Do you get a soft-box light or one with a reflector? Do you use spotlights or a work light from Sears or Home Depot? Once you have decided on which lights to purchase, you need to know how to place them and how far away from you they need to be.

Halogen warning: They generate massive amounts of heat. In contrast, fluorescent lights are cool to the touch, but you have to know what temperature each of the lights generate and how that will affect the settings within your video camera. Each type of bulb that you choose will create different skin tones, because different bulbs take up different spectrums of light.

How many different lights do you need in order to illuminate yourself? In ideal circumstances, I personally use five lights to illuminate myself. Other times I will use one or two.

Placement of lights: No, this is not rocket science, but then again, it's not as simple as turning on spotlights and then shooting video. WARNING: Never shoot video near a window. Why not? Your video camera will think that the light coming through the window is a light source. What's the big deal? When your camera recognizes a light source, it automatically makes everything else dark. So although you may think that your nice picture window in the corner office of your high-rise office building is beautiful, rest assured that shooting video in front of it will destroy your video entirely. If you have a video camera with manual settings and understand how and why to use them, you have the ability to minimize the drastic effect that the light from a window source will have by adjusting your settings.

Understanding and mastering video, audio, and lighting is only half of the technique equation for you to become a master videographer. Throughout this process, you must continually ask yourself whether you want to spend your time, energy, and resources to become an expert videographer. Put another way, would you rather be spending time with your family and enjoying your hobbies, or would you prefer to learn how to shoot, edit, and publish your marketing videos?

THE EDITING NIGHTMARE

Once you have mastered each piece of video equipment, you then have to understand the entire process of how to upload the video to your computer and how to edit it. Sounds simple again, right? It can be if you decide to cut corners and not do much editing at all. I will tell you, after creating over 600 videos to market my own solo practice, it is virtually impossible to create an entire video clip without making mistakes. Lawyers who speak for a living think they can easily get up in front of the camera and ramble for 2–3 minutes and create a perfect video clip on the first take. Even with 23 years as a practicing trial lawyer and years of experience as a video producer, video editor, and video publisher, I will tell you that I have yet to see any attorney create perfect videos in one take.

How long does video editing take?

For a 2 to 3 minute final video clip, it will take me 30–45 minutes to edit. Another 15 minutes to add graphics, add music, color correct, and sound correct. Then it must be rendered, which takes 5–15 minutes. Once rendered, it must be converted to a QuickTime movie file. That can take anywhere from 30 minutes to two hours. Then, the video must be compressed, and that takes about five minutes. Total elapsed time: 2–3 hours for just *one* video clip!

As a master video editor you will have to learn how to put together a concise, tight video segment that gets your message across without putting your viewer to sleep. You will have an extremely difficult time cutting out words that you uttered that you believe your viewer absolutely needs to hear.

BEST-PRACTICE TIP

One of the best pieces of advice I can give you is that if you want to create great quality video, you must edit and edit and edit again. Your 10- to 15-minute legal dissertation on the tax code or some obscure municipal regulation may be fascinating to you and your colleagues. However, I guarantee that your viewers will not watch it. If you fail to provide your viewers with direct answers to their questions, you will lose them forever.

Remember this: When you argue an appeal or present an argument to the court and the judge asks you a direct question, you give a direct answer. Do the same with video. Don't dawdle and don't ramble. Make your point and move on.

In addition to editing your video masterpiece, you must learn how to create intro and exit graphics. You will need to learn how to insert and use intro and exit music. Make sure you learn how to fade music in and out. Otherwise your music will abruptly end as your video starts. That is awkward and uncool.

You must learn how to color correct your video and tweak your audio settings. You need to create graphics that tell people who you are and how to contact you. That's not all.

You need to process and "render" your video in order to make it come together in a usable video format. You need to learn what video settings will get you crystal-clear video. The automatic settings on most video editing programs are not always ideal. How many frames per second will you use? 25, 29, 30? You must learn why those settings make a difference. You also have to understand what format to put your video in. Understanding the technical settings makes the difference between having crystal-clear video and video that is pixelated and not watchable. Flash format or QuickTime format? What about HTML5 format and mobile formats? Are they all compatible with website and mobile devices? Not all are.

Once you've rendered your video, you are left with a huge video file that takes a tremendous amount of space on your hard drive. You need massive hard-drive memory, video graphics, and video processors on your computer since video editing is a resource hog. Once your video is complete, you're still not done. You must now use another program to properly compress the file so you can upload it to your website and the video-sharing sites.

IT'S TIME TO PUBLISH AND SYNDICATE YOUR VIDEOS

This part is easy. All you have to do is spend the time to upload your video to 30 different video-sharing sites individually.

Don't forget to upload to Facebook, Twitter and LinkedIn as well. That will take you days to accomplish. You may have heard of different website companies that allow you to upload your video once and blast the video out to multiple video-sharing sites. Two of the better-known video blast companies are Traffic Geyser and TubeMogul. Traffic Geyser is a paid service with an à-la-carte menu that can get expensive if you want all the bells and whistles. TubeMogul is mostly free for personal use, and they charge a fee for business use.

Do you know how to optimize your videos in order to increase the chances that a viewer will find your video? Do you know how to create compelling headlines and descriptions that people want to read? Do you know the difference between keywords and tags? If your videos are not properly optimized, nobody will find or watch your videos no matter how great your content is.

"I can figure out how to optimize my videos on my own," said one attorney. Of course you can. You can learn how to do all this on your own. The question is: do you really want to spend all your time learning how to do this well? And if that's what you want to do, then I encourage you to do it, because it is a lot of fun. However, most attorneys simply don't have the desire, inclination, or time to learn how to be a master videographer, video editor, and video distributor.

CHAPTER 18

HOW LONG IS THE ENTIRE VIDEO PROCESS TO DO IT ON YOUR OWN?

1.	Set up equipment	15 minutes
2.	Shoot video	1 hour
3.	Take down equipment	15 minutes
4.	Load/transcode video onto computer (approx.)	1 hour
5.	Edit video clip	2–3 hours (approx.)
6.	Upload video online and optimize	30 minutes
7.	Create blog post and article	1 hour
8.	Use social network	10 minutes
	Total time (approximately)	5–6 hours

Even after you have uploaded your videos to your website and video-sharing sites, you still are not yet done. You must now tell the world about each new video that you create. You must use your social network to tell people about your new videos, among many other things that you must do to get the word out. Failure to do so will mean that your videos will likely not generate many views, or many calls to your office.

WHY ARE YOU CREATING VIDEO?

Your entire goal of creating video is to make that phone ring. If it's not happening for you, then you must reassess why it's not working.

Don't have the time or desire to do all this? No problem. I have a solution.

For those lawyers who say, "I don't want to learn how to do any of this stuff, I just want someone to do it all for me," I say, "I have the perfect solution for you."

As a practicing New York medical malpractice trial lawyer in the trenches every day, I created a "done-for-you solution" so that you don't have to do anything other than show up and start talking. I call it my *Total Online Video Success program*. It's a way for you to create six months of video in one day by shooting video at your office. The great thing is that you don't have to learn how to become a videographer, video editor, or video distributor. We do it all for you. Lawyers who value their time recognize that there are experts they can use to help solve their video marketing problem.

As the only veteran medical malpractice trial lawyer in the country who's also an experienced video producer who helps lawyers create compelling video, I have a unique understanding of who your ideal client is. Understanding what will compel an online viewer to pick up the phone and call you is critical and most video companies don't fully understand this.

THE LEVEL OF PROFESSIONALISM AND HELP THAT YOU GET FROM GERRY AND LAWYERS VIDEO STUDIO... IT HAS BEEN THE BEST

"Hello. I'm Laura Claveran. I'm a bankruptcy attorney, as well as a personal injury attorney in Long Beach, California. I've got to tell you today in this day and age and this terrible economy, you really have to stay up with what's new and what's effective in terms of advertising.

Before I hired the Lawyers Video Studio and Gerry Oginski, I searched for and in fact contracted other companies. But the level of professionalism and help that you get from Gerry and Lawyers Video Studio...it has been the best. They work with me in a lot of the preparation for the video shoot. They give me suggestions on how to improve my content and how to approach it. Gerry's very knowledgeable in how to make things work.

I feel like we, as attorneys, have all this information in our head and we feel like we can just get in front of the camera and tell the whole world how smart we are with all the fancy terms that we use. In reality, Gerry is absolutely correct. You have to keep things simple. Just keep it simple and appeal to the layperson. Doing it in a series of educational videos is the best approach.

I am very thankful. I also wanted to let you know that the video shoot day was pretty much as they indicated it was. They give you an agenda ahead of time and they stick to that agenda. They were very punctual. Scott was my producer and David was the assistant producer and they were both wonderful and very knowledgeable and very good with all the technical aspects of producing video. So I'm very thankful to Lawyers Video Studio. I'm glad I searched for Gerry on the Internet and found him. Just like we hope that our clients will search for us on the Internet and find us. Thank you."

Laura Claveran, Esq.
Bankruptcy Attorney
Claveran Law Firm
5199 Pacific Coast Highway, Suite 508
Long Beach, California 90804
Telephone: 562-396-5291

SCAN WITH YOUR SMARTPHONE TO WATCH & LISTEN TO LAURA CLAVERAN'S VIDEO.

Step Away from the Wall and Turn On Your Lights

This sounds almost like a state trooper pulling you over at 2 a.m. on the main highway. However, make no mistake, if you fail to follow the directive above, your videos will look awful.

I have repeatedly stated that your viewers expect to see a seamless and technically proficient video that simply provides them with an education. They don't want to see poor lighting, poor audio, or a poor video frame that looks like your five-year-old was holding the camera. The bar has risen in terms of what constitutes a high-quality video. Just because you are shooting in high-definition does not mean you will have a compelling video or a great quality video.

All too often I see attorneys sitting in a chair against the wall when shooting video. Or I see lawyers standing against a wall while shooting video. Let me say clearly in a loud booming voice, *step away from the wall!*

THE WALL IS NOT YOUR FRIEND

It's not just that you look awkward up against the wall. By sitting or standing against the wall, the camera captures a two-dimensional and flat image of you. There's no depth behind you for the camera to capture. There's no contrast between you and the wall or furniture immediately behind you. This puts you in a decidedly two-dimensional, flat image. Just like we tell our clients that the defense lawyers at a deposition are not your friend, the same holds true for the wall and your video. *The wall is not your friend; stay away from the wall.* In fact, you would do well to separate yourself from the wall by about 4–5 feet.

This will give your video some depth in your background that you can illuminate as you see fit. That brings me to the second part of the title.

AND ON THE FIRST DAY GOD SAID, "LET THERE BE LIGHT!"

Do not use the available light in your home or office to create your video. You must have supplemental lights that illuminate your face and remove shadows. If your viewer cannot see you clearly, they will wonder why. If your video is not illuminated well, your viewer will not spend the time to find out what your message is.

You need at a minimum two soft boxes. You should place them about 6–8 feet away from you, to the right and left sides of you, at about a 45° angle from where you are sitting. This will eliminate the shadows on your face.

WHAT I USE TO ILLUMINATE

I personally like to use four to five lights when shooting video. In addition to soft-box lights, I will also have an overhead light known as a boom pole that illuminates the top of my head. This is also known as a hair light and is used to provide contrast between the top of my head and my background. I will often use additional lights to light up my background. Again, this is done to liven up the background and create contrast between me and what is behind me.

SET YOUR WHITE BALANCE

Remember, no matter what device you use and no matter what camera you use, you must always set your white balance before pressing the record button. If you fail to take this little step that will take you 10 seconds, you will likely ruin the color of your video every single time. Most lawyers rely on the automatic white balance setting on the camera. If you are shooting video outdoors, you will likely get good color. However, when shooting video indoors there are different lighting elements that will affect the color of your video.

A fluorescent bulb will change the color differently than an incandescent bulb. An overcast, gray day may shade the color of your video more than you would prefer. The problem with automatic white balance is that your camera averages what it believes are the correct colors.

In reality, the color you see in your camera viewfinder may also be different than what you see when you play back your video during the editing process. Although you can try and change color in the postproduction editing process, it is always preferable to properly set your color when shooting your video. Simply take a piece of white poster board or white paper and hold it in front of you. Go into your camera settings and press the custom white balance setting. Zoom all the way in so that the entire viewfinder only shows the poster board or paper. Press the white balance setting. Once set, zoom out and you're now ready to shoot your video.

What you have just done is told the camera what color is actually white. It then automatically resets all the other colors in the room. You are now on the road to creating great quality video. *Make sure you step away from the wall and turn on your lights.*

I DON'T HAVE A TOLERANCE FOR PEOPLE WHO BULLSHIT. WHAT I APPRECIATE ABOUT GERRY IS THAT HE DOESN'T WASTE MY TIME. HE GETS RIGHT TO IT

"In the morning, I was anxious and wanted to get more done. I felt like I wasn't accomplishing as much as I wanted to accomplish. Throughout  the day my confidence grew. You're doing video after video, so you're starting to feel more comfortable with the process.

I like to think of myself as a straight shooter. I don't have a whole lot of tolerance for people who bullshit. So, what I appreciate about what Gerry does is that he doesn't waste a whole lot of my time. He gets right to it and helps me focus on improving the video and focusing on delivering the message quickly and effectively. I really appreciate that.

Well, obviously the biggest problem in shooting these videos is not necessarily the content that you know, it's how do you do it? How do you present the information in a manner that is going to be effective? You got to keep it simple and obviously Gerry helped me deliver that in keeping it simple.

Do I think somebody without a law background could have done this? Yeah, I do.

Do I think it helped that you have a law background? Absolutely. You can talk my language, and you've been doing this long enough that you can also talk the language that I need to talk into the camera. So you're basically dual language and you can translate from one to the other.

There was a couple times today when I needed to speak legal language in order to get my point across and you helped me translate that into language that people can understand. I'm interested in generating more revenue. Obviously, just buying a camera and putting on the lights and flipping the switch and getting in front of a camera isn't enough. You need a coach. Somebody that can independently and objectively look at what you're doing and give you advice to make sure you do it right.

This is obviously not a very natural thing to be talking into a camera versus talking to a person. You can't gauge their reaction in what the camera is doing. The camera doesn't really react to you.

When I talk to people, I like to have a two-way conversation even if I'm the one talking and the other person is responding at least non-verbally. That is telling me what they're thinking about what I'm saying. The tricky thing about a camera is that doesn't happen. You just have a cold stare right back at you and you don't get the input you get when you're having a two-way conversation. So having a coach is critical.

Eric Engel, Esq.
Bankruptcy & Divorce Attorney
Engel Law Group
One Union Square
600 University St., Suite 1904
Seattle, Washington
206-438-4629

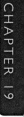

**SCAN WITH YOUR
SMARTPHONE** TO
WATCH & LISTEN TO
ERIC ENGEL'S VIDEO.

Why You Need to Shoot Video in Your Office

I have created educational video in my basement, in my backyard, at the pool club, on vacation in the Bahamas, in Florida, while at marketing seminars, and many other places. However, the most important place you can ever shoot video *is in your law office.*

There are some lawyers who believe that their office is not worthy of being shown on video. Others are worried that the size of their office will diminish the impression or the perception of their legal ability. Yet others are proud to show off where they work.

The overwhelming incentive for shooting video in your office has nothing to do with the size, shape, color, or location of your office. It has nothing to do with whether your office is clean or messy. It has nothing to do with whether you have a quiet office or a busy office.

The underlying reason and purpose for creating video in your office has a deep, psychological purpose that, once I share it with you, you'll immediately recognize how powerful it is. Do not get me wrong. I am not a fan of psychobabble or psychology. I have no specialized training in the field of psychology, but I have learned a great deal about how psychology influences how viewers perceive us and how they act upon our messages. In that regard, I have become a quick student.

Let me explain to you why you need to shoot video in your office.

A GENTLEMAN ARRIVES IN MY OFFICE

A gentleman called me with a potential new wrongful death case. On the phone, after my brief screening call, I invited him and his family into my office to further evaluate their potential matter.

As an aside, you should have just recognized one important marketing tip that you should all be doing. You should be qualifying every prospect on the telephone before inviting them into your office to spend an hour with you chatting about their case. *You must require that your prospects prove themselves worthy of hiring you.* That is a topic for another day, but that method of thinking will revolutionize the way you evaluate and take in new cases.

Let's get back to this gentleman who had a possible wrongful death case. During our 3-minute screening call, he told me he found one of the videos I created about wrongful death that was virtually identical to the scenario that he found himself in that day. Probing further, I learned that he might have a viable case, and I scheduled an appointment for him and his family.

On the appointed day and time, a distinguished looking gentleman walked into my office with an overcoat and a cane accompanied by two of his family members. He immediately thrust out his hand and introduced himself. I did the same. His next words were startling. *"I feel like I already know you."*

Before choosing his seat, he quickly looked around my office and remarked to me, *"I feel as if I have already been here before."*

I knew full well that I had never met the the man in my life. I was also fully aware that he had never stepped foot in my office before. Yet here was an intelligent, distinguished man who told me, in the span of 10 seconds, everything that validated what I do with video.

He felt as if he already knew me.

It turns out that he watched about 12 of my videos on wrongful death. He was fascinated and eager to learn more. He immediately notified his family members that they should go online and start watching my videos. Those videos prompted this gentleman to pick up the phone and call me. My videos began the process of establishing a bond with this viewer that got him to recognize I had information he needed to know. My content was engaging and of great interest to him. He got to know me and like me and began to trust me before he ever met me.

The reason you want to shoot video in your office is so that your viewers can become familiar with and feel comfortable with you and your law office setting, so when they arrive in your office they feel as if they have already been there. It is a déjà-vu feeling to walk into a place that you've seen many times before but yet have never stepped foot in. From a psychological standpoint, you no longer have to overcome the trust hurdle that so many of us attorneys have to deal with on a daily basis.

MY RECOMMENDATION

My recommendation is to create video in your office. Let them see your desk, let them see your possessions that sit on your desk. Let them see your conference room and where you work. Throw open your office doors and warmly invite your viewer in to join you. Your potential clients likely have never been inside a lawyer's office before. Why not show them where you work and how you work so that they feel comfortable when they do show up in your office. From a psychological standpoint this is an extremely powerful suggestion and changes the dynamics from a prospect deciding whether to hire you, into one who actually begs you to be their lawyer.

When a new prospect comes into my office, they already come in prequalified, and they literally beg me to take their case. No longer do I have to spend time convincing them that I'm trustworthy and that I am the right one to handle their problems. By the time they arrive in my office, they have already determined in their own mind that I am the right lawyer for them. This is a dramatic and revolutionary change from how the attorney selection process used to work for me.

If you want to make this happen for yourself, make sure you shoot video in your office.

SHOULD I USE GREEN SCREEN IN MY OFFICE?

Lawyers often ask me when creating do-it-yourself video whether they should use a green screen in their office to create special effects. I ask them why they want to create green-screen video when shooting in their office. Most lawyers simply think it will help drive traffic to their video. They don't have a clear idea of how that will happen, but somehow they feel that, from a technology standpoint, creating a green-screen video while sitting in their office will help.

These same lawyers fail to recognize that during the postproduction process of editing your videos you must now put an image behind you or some type of animation that will be your background. Many lawyers who attempt to use green-screen animation and effects get awful results. The attempt is good and their intention is clear. However, the implementation is where they run into a problem.

Even experienced video producers are often challenged to create great quality green-screen video. It is a time-intensive process that can be extremely frustrating for the novice and intermediate video editor. If you want to take the time and effort to learn how to do it well, there is a huge learning curve.

I'm going to share with you a recommendation that you should take to heart when debating whether to create your own do-it-yourself green-screen studio effects. Before I give you my recommendation, I want to tell you, from a psychological perspective, why it is more important *not* to use green screen in your office.

If your videos are compelling, your consumers will likely watch multiple videos you have created before deciding they want more information from you. Then if you have given them a compelling reason to call, when that person walks into your office, they will immediately feel comfortable with you.

If instead of using your natural surroundings in your office you decide to use green-screen studio effects, you must now insert some image or animation instead. The choice of what to insert in your background can be overwhelming. My recommendation is not to use cliché images of courthouses, gavels, gowns, Lady Liberty, eagles, or flags. Those are clearly outdated and serve no purpose. Instead, focus on the content and not on the technical issues that can easily distract if not done properly.

You will be pleasantly surprised when a potential new client comes into your office, after having watched many of your videos, when they tell you for the very first time, "I feel like I have already been here, even though I know I've never stepped foot in this office before today." That is when you know that your video had the desired effect of creating a bond with your viewer and getting them to like you, trust you, and want to chat with you, simply by virtue of creating a compelling, educational message.

If you want to learn more about how powerful and compelling educational video can be for lawyers, I encourage you to join me in a free educational webinar about Secrets of Video in the Age of YouTube (www.LawyersVideoStudio.com).

SCAN WITH YOUR SMARTPHONE
TO WATCH & LISTEN TO A FREE
EDUCATIONAL WEBINAR ABOUT SECRETS
OF VIDEO IN THE AGE OF YOUTUBE.

Most Video Production Companies Can't Help You

Here are 10 reasons why most video production companies can't help you create video:

1. THEY DON'T KNOW WHO YOUR IDEAL CLIENT IS

Most video producers are not trial attorneys. Unless they have specialized knowledge about your area of law, they may not have a good understanding of your client base and who your perfect client is. If they don't know who your ideal client is, how can they help you create video that will compel a viewer to call you?

2. THEY ARE NOT TRIAL ATTORNEYS WHO ARE IN THE TRENCHES EVERY DAY

You practice law every day. You know the law. You know what type of client comes to you. You know what questions they ask and what problems they have. If your video producer and production company are not lawyers who actively practice law, how are they going to know how to help you create content that will compel a viewer to click on your headline and watch your entire video?

3. THEY COPY WHAT HAS WORKED FOR TV AND TRANSFER IT TO VIDEO

The problem with TV advertising for attorneys is that the message has always been truncated because of time limitations. Nobody wants to hear you shout to the world, "Come to me because I'm great and I have 30 seconds to tell you I'm great." TV-style marketing ads simply don't work well for attorney online video.

4. THEY COPY THE SAME STYLE FOR EVERY BUSINESS

There are very few online video production companies that only do attorney video. Most create video for businesses and occasionally for attorneys. What works for small businesses does not necessarily work for attorney video, and vice-versa.

5. THEY DON'T UNDERSTAND WHAT YOUR ONLINE VIEWER IS LOOKING FOR

If your video producer doesn't know the details of your area of law and who your ideal client is, chances are they may also not know what your ideal clients are looking for online. If your video production company doesn't know what an online viewer is looking for when searching for an attorney who practices in your specialty, how can they help you fashion content that will interest your viewer and, importantly, get that viewer to convert to a caller?

6. THEY MAY NOT UNDERSTAND HOW TO CREATE COMPELLING CONTENT

One problem with attorney video today is that most of it is boring. If your video company tells you to create content without knowing whether it's interesting enough to get viewers to call, you may be wasting your resources. Most good, experienced online video companies can create good quality video. That's not the issue. The problem is getting a video producer who understands you, your clients, your practice area, and what information your viewers want, *not* what your video producer wants you to tell them.

7. THEY WANT YOU TO TALK ABOUT YOURSELF

If this is what your video producer tells you, then you should run and demand your money back. Why? Because *nobody* wants to hear you talk about yourself. Your online viewer does not care about you. Ever. Only after they get to know you, like you, and trust you do they want to learn about you. But not before then.

8. THEY WANT YOU TO TALK ABOUT YOUR CREDENTIALS

See #7 above.

9. THEY WANT YOU TO TALK ABOUT YOUR LAW FIRM

Nobody cares how long your firm has been in business. Nobody cares about all those diplomas on the wall. Nobody cares if you were on moot court or law review or where you went to law school. Nobody. The *only* thing an online viewer wants to know is how you can help solve *their* problem. That's it.

10. THEY DON'T UNDERSTAND THAT YOUR VIEWERS DON'T CARE ABOUT YOU

Creating video has nothing to do with you. Literally. It's all about your clients. Most video companies fail to understand that.

SHOULD YOU HIRE THE "LOWEST BID" VIDEO COMPANY?

You can call three different video production companies and go with the one that gives you the lowest price. Remember what I said earlier? You will get what you pay for with video production. There is no substitute for having a video marketing company that is tried and true and has perfected and tested techniques such as the ones I personally use to successfully market my solo practice.

VIDEO PRODUCTION COMPANY OR VIDEO MARKETING COMPANY?

There is a difference between a video production company and a video marketing company. Understanding the difference will help you find a company to create video for you if you are not inclined to create video on your own.

A video production company is one that is familiar with creating video and putting it online. They will have many years experience doing this. They will have a video producer and camera crew. They will have video editors who can create amazing special effects and graphics. They will know all there is to know about video and how to upload it online.

A video marketing company will have all that too. The difference is that a video marketing company helps you create a video marketing campaign and not just a series of videos.

A video marketing company is one that helps you, guides you, and coaches you to create great, compelling content. Such a company understands who you are and who your ideal clients are. This type of company recognizes why your online viewers are searching for an attorney and knows how to create content they need and want.

A video marketing company helps you market your videos, promotes your videos, and teaches you how to use social media to maximize the chances your videos will be found.

A video marketing company encourages you with monthly coaching calls to use your video content in many different ways.

Make sure you understand what type of company you're talking to when deciding who to hire for your lawyer videos.

VIDEO METRICS FOR LAWYERS: TOTALLY USELESS

A video company tells you they can track everything that happens with your video. They have fancy graphs, reports, and analytics. They can tell you what page your viewer came from, where they clicked, and how long they watched. They can tell what page a viewer clicked to, and whether they clicked on a link in the video.

What they don't tell you is that it's all meaningless. Yes, you read that correctly. Useless, needless garbage that does nothing to help you.

Here's why. Analytics and metrics can be very useful to analyze what's working and what's not. This works well with websites and blogs. You can identify what needs to be modified and then easily make changes to reflect what's working and what isn't.

Video, on the other hand, is different.

Remember, the only reason you look at metrics is to analyze what's working. If a video isn't generating callers or doing as well as you expected, what *should* you do? The answer is either to modify the video or take it down and put up a new one. The reality is that no video production company is going to come back into your office to modify a video just because of your video metrics. It's simply not cost effective to do that. Nor is it cost effective for you to shoot just one video over again because your metrics show it's not doing well.

If your video production company is not going to modify the video with you, then what's the purpose of generating all those high-falootin' (fancy slang word), snazzy-looking pie charts and graphs? The answer: there is *no* purpose. That's why all those video metrics are *useless*. If any video production company starts telling you about their great software and analytics that track your video metrics, I suggest running in the other direction, and fast.

I will share with you the *only* metric I care about, ever. Are you ready? The only metric that is important is *how many people call you as a result of watching your video*. That's it! No other video metric matters. Of course you also want to track how many of those callers you actually took on as clients and what results you achieved for those clients.

Now you know the secret to video metrics.

Important Tips You Need to Know

Here are five video tips for what you need to know, and importantly, what you don't:

TIP #1

What you should never include in your video: yourself!

Let me repeat that. Do not talk about yourself.

Have you ever been to a party and you mistakenly ask someone what they do for a living, and for the next 10 minutes all they do is talk about themselves? I have, and can tell you it gets pretty tiring listening to someone talk about how great they are. Or maybe you've been to a lawyer marketing event where the lawyer is trying to tell you how busy he is and how many projects he's involved in.

Do you really care? Think about viewers who come to your website looking for answers to their questions. In my opinion, if you have a website that says you're a lawyer, a potential client presumes that you know what you are talking about. If you give them a reason to doubt you, they will. Same with juries.

Enough generalization, let's get right down to it. A potential client looking for answers to their legal problem does not want to hear about you. They want to hear about them. They want to hear how you can help *them*. I guarantee that if you start talking about how wonderful you are and how great you are the viewer will be turned off and jump away from your website, never to call you. Why? Because the viewer doesn't care about you. Remember, they are the one with the problem. That's why they are doing a Google search to find an attorney who can best answer their questions.

Here's a quick exercise. Go to YouTube and do a search for attorneys in your specialty. Watch their videos. Then ask yourself these four important questions:

1. What information is this attorney trying to provide to me?

2. What have I learned from this attorney video?

3. What makes this attorney different from every other attorney in this field?

4. If I needed an attorney, would this be the one I called and why?

In all likelihood, the lawyer in the video will fail to identify why you should call him instead of his competitor down the street. It's the same thing with almost all yellow pages ads. Simply move around the law firm name and number, and a potential client cannot tell one ad apart from the other.

Caveat: if you are the best attorney in your state and have achieved precedent-setting cases and verdicts, then you should do everything possible to tell the world about those achievements.

In my opinion, those videos should be done by interview. Interview the clients or, even better, your adversary—to get a true, unbiased opinion of your abilities. It is so much better to have someone else describe how incredible your trial skills are than for you to tell a viewer directly. Testimonials, if done correctly, and in accordance with your state's ethics rules, have an incredible effect upon a website viewer.

Most attorney videos give a resume of where they went to college and law school, what bar associations they participate in, what awards they've received, how long they've been in practice... the standard junk that all bar associations say you're required to give. (It reminds me of the movies where a downed pilot is interrogated and the only information he is obligated to give is his name, rank, and serial number.)

So what?

What good does that do for a potential viewer?

Nothing, in my opinion. Every lawyer has the same qualifications to a certain extent. Do you really think a layman can differentiate a law degree from one law school over another, except maybe for a top-tier school? Do they really care whether you were on law review or moot court? No. They just want to know that you can help them with their pressing legal problem. How does that distinguish you from every other lawyer? They all went to law school. If they're practicing, they all passed the bar exam (at least that's the theory, and hopefully the law too). So how does a viewer determine whether you are the "right one" for their problem? Not by listening to you talk about yourself.

Why do these lawyers spend so much time and effort to talk about themselves and give a "video resume"? Because of the advice by the company that is creating the video. Some "marketing expert" has told them that if they do not tell people about their background, then they will not seem credible. That's nonsense. However, if you want to continue to rely on the same pitch that the video rep gives you and that the yellow pages rep gives you, then by all means, drink the Kool-aid.

What to Include in Your Video

An attorney called me recently to ask what topics he should include in his newsletter that he intended to send to his list of clients and friends. He didn't believe me when I told him what he should put in his newsletter.

I told him, "Don't put anything about law in it." He thought I was joking. I wasn't. If you think I'm wrong, why don't you ask your Aunt Silvia, whom you sent your last newsletter to, whether she needs to know what a "right of subrogation" is. Ask your neighbor down the street—an owner of a bagel store—whether he finds legal updates about whistleblower cases useful for his business. Better yet, ask your best friend for her opinion about whether that new case on mergers and acquisitions will help her job as a sales clerk in a clothing store. These people don't want to hear about the law unless they need a lawyer to solve their problems. The same for the attorney videos. Unless they're looking for a specific topic, your video will never be watched.

Who Is Your Target Audience?

The elderly? Small businesses? Injured victims? Fortune-500 CEOs? You have to know who your audience is before you can even begin to create your videos.

Next time you get an attorney newsletter, I can almost guarantee that they'll spend most of the time talking about law, or about themselves. Why? Because someone has told them to show their friends and family how smart and erudite they are about their area of law. Not a bad idea initially, until you begin to look at newsletters from a nonlegal perspective.

When all the marketing types are saying the same thing, you get the sense that if you deviate from what they're saying you might be doing something wrong. It's just like the yellow pages again. The yellow pages rep tells you that if you get a bigger ad, the potential client will call you. Get color, get fancy graphics, spend more money. So what if you're 30 pages from the front, you'll still get calls. Yeah sure. Keep dreaming. Don't you think every lawyer gets the same pitch? There's nothing to differentiate you from anyone else in that thick book with lots of phone numbers and photos of crashed cars, big gavels, mean-looking attorneys, and the same clichés you hear over and over.

Talking about yourself generates abundant video time for the website company, or billable hours for those of you used to counting your hours and minutes. The more time you spend talking about things that will not cause a client to call you is, in my mind, simply a waste of your time and money.

TIP #2

Do not talk about how difficult your area of law is.

If you deal in a difficult or arcane area of law, do not tell viewers how complex it is. It's a waste of your breath, and a lost opportunity to let a viewer know you have the ability to handle their case. This is analogous to a trial lawyer giving an opening statement where he wastes five minutes explaining to the jury what an opening statement is and how a trial is conducted. Stop telling your viewer about how difficult these cases are, and start showing your viewer that you know what you are talking about.

Repeatedly, I hear lawyers from all over the country say this in their videos: "I handle medical malpractice cases, and these are the most difficult and complex cases around. These complex cases are so difficult because... yada yada..." Your viewer does not want to hear that their legal quagmire is so complex and difficult that even you, the brilliant legal whiz kid, will have trouble solving it. They want to hear that you have the answers to their questions! If you tell them how hard these cases are, then I guarantee you, they will go to someone who doesn't explain in big, bold letters how tough these cases are. These viewers want answers, not excuses!

TIP #3

Here's what 99 percent of attorneys do not include in their videos: information! (This is a million-dollar video tip.)

In case you have not realized it, we're in the Internet age. It is the information age. Potential clients go online to get... yes... you can say it, come on, say it with me... *information.* The more information you can give them, the greater chance you will have that you will be seen as *the expert* in your field of law. They get to know you through your informative video. By the time they are done watching your video, you have educated your viewer, and he likely has more questions to ask about his particular matter. That is what prompts a call to your office.

Caveat: I am not advocating giving any legal advice in your video. I do not want you to run afoul of any ethics rules in your state, nor do I want you establishing any attorney-client relationship with what you say in your video.

"What then am I supposed to put in my video if you're telling me to put information in the video, but not give legal advice?"

Give general information about the process.

What do I mean?

Explain how cases work. Most people are unfamiliar with the mechanics of how a lawsuit for their problem works. For example, I created a video where I explain in detail how a medical malpractice lawsuit in New York works. I started by explaining what an attorney does to evaluate their potential case, described the mechanics of getting an expert opinion, the mechanics of drafting a summons and complaint, getting an answer, setting up a preliminary conference with the court, depositions… and on and on it goes. Viewers eat this up. Why? Because *nobody* gives them this information anywhere else, except after they've made an appointment and stepped into a lawyer's office.

If you are a trusts-and-estates attorney, how about explaining what probate is? If there is a contested will, explain the process about what information you need and what the court requires. If you handle real-estate closings, explain what escrow is and why an engineer needs to examine the house. Talk about going to contract. A potential homeowner who has never purchased a home before will appreciate the education. Remember, you are not giving legal advice. Your goal is to give viewers sufficient general information so they want more answers to their questions.

TIP #4

Keep your video short, but not too short, and not too long.

"What does that mean?" It means you want it longer than a 30-second commercial. It means you want it longer than one minute. It means you need enough time to convey the information that your viewer needs, whether that takes two minutes or five to six minutes. If the information is relevant, then your viewer will spend the time to watch.

"What about a 10-minute video?" My advice is, that is too long. Think about your attention span and how long you will sit to watch a video clip. Unless you have a burning interest in what you are watching, a few minutes maximum is all you will do. My suggestion is to do multiple videos, each a few minutes in length.

I prefer to keep my videos and those of my video clients at 2–3 minutes. That's my sweet spot.

TIP #5

You must use interesting headlines.

Seems simple, right? Not really. There are editors in every newspaper across this country who spend endless amounts of time coming up with headlines that will catch a reader's attention. Once a viewer has passed on the headline, that article or video is gone forever, never to be viewed by that person. You must come up with a short headline that telegraphs your topic and creates immediate interest.

Next time you are in the supermarket, look at the headlines in the tabloids. Those cheesy headlines attract everyone's interest. It doesn't mean you'll pick up the magazine to read the article, but I guarantee you that you'll be tempted.

Here's an example of a headline I used in a video that became extremely popular: "Questions Never to Ask at a Deposition."

Why was it so popular? Because most attorneys know that there are very few questions that you cannot ask at a deposition. The headline was a tease. In fact, in my video I clearly explained that in New York there are very few limitations on what can be asked.

"Who creates the headlines?" You do. Do not rely on your video company to do it for you. Be creative. Look at the newspaper you read each day. Look to seek what headlines catch your attention. Adapt some of those headlines for your videos.

The Benefit of Video

The key is to get in on the ground floor now, because the longer you wait to do videos, the longer it will take you to overcome your competitors who have learned how to do this.

Virginia personal injury trial lawyer Ben Glass, who teaches marketing to lawyers all over the country says, "Gerry Oginski is one of the few lawyers who really 'get it' in terms of taking creative marketing ideas and combining them with the latest technology in order to 'start a conversation' with potential clients. It's no longer good enough to just have a message that you 'shout' out to consumers via the yellow pages, TV, radio, or the Internet. The big edge that Gerry has over the competition is that his marketing style allows consumers to get to 'know' him before they even pick up the phone. His use of video on his website is phenomenal. I can't tell you how valuable it is for Gerry to be dominating not only the search engine terms for 'regular' web marketing but also to be all over YouTube, Google Video and other video sites with his messages."

Video Marketing for Lawyers

VIDEO TIP #1

Educate. Do not sell.

This is the most important video tip I can give. This tip will save you thousands of dollars and endless amounts of time. In fact, this tip is so useful that I should have you make a donation to my favorite charity. I'm serious.

If you do not know the difference between educating and selling, walk into a car showroom and ask yourself whether the salesman is trying to sell you a car or trying to educate you about the cars he sells.

If you come across as a salesman, you will lose all your viewers, and you probably will not get any calls. The reason why attorney video works so well is because it is the best way to educate a potential client and at the same time have them get to know you.

Why does that help? Once a viewer gets to know you, they begin to trust you. They will listen to you. They want to hear what you have to say. If you try to make a sale to your viewer from your short video clip, they will click on the next video, never to pick up the phone and call you. Your video should be to teach and educate. Not sell. By teaching, you show that you are an expert. A salesman is someone to be avoided.

VIDEO TIP #2

Talk about what you know best.

When a potential client comes into your office, they ask the same questions every potential client asks. These form the basis of your FAQs. Well, here's what you talk about in your videos.

"How long will my lawsuit take?"

"How much is my case worth?"

"How much time do I have to file a lawsuit against a municipal hospital in New York City?"

"What documents do I need to bring to you?"

Ask the question in your title, then answer the question in your video.

VIDEO TIP #3

Make your video about 2-3 minutes long.

Some will be shorter, some longer. Many video companies think that video clips less than one minute are useful. I disagree. But I think you do yourself a big disservice by only creating a series of video clips that are less than one minute each.

Why?

Because video is king on the Internet. It is the best media available, at the lowest cost, to get your marketing message out to the world. All other media limited your ability to explain to a viewer how your expertise could help an injured victim with a particular problem. That has accounted for one reason why attorneys developed such a bad reputation.

Attorney ads have been spoofed and ridiculed since lawyers started advertising in 1973 when the U.S. Supreme Court said lawyers could advertise. Saturday Night Live created lawyer commercials that were at once funny and satirical. Every late night comedy host has ridiculed lawyer ads. Why were lawyer ads so pathetic? Because the media we used to get our message out was severely truncated.

In the limited space of our yellow pages ads, we couldn't explain anything. A classified ad did not allow us to explain how we were different from anybody else. Television ads simply yelled at you, and as my friend and fellow trial lawyer

Ben Glass says, "These ads just shouted at you. They all tried to out shout each other." An injured victim looking for a lawyer with traditional advertising media couldn't tell how one attorney was different or better than any other.

Video allows you to show viewers how you are different. It allows you to show a viewer you are confident and know what you're talking about. It allows you to show you are a legal expert without ever saying, "Come to me because I'm the best!" If you have not realized it yet, video is the future of attorney marketing online.

Those attorneys who recognize the benefits of getting onto video now, have a better chance of getting their videos ranked higher in the search engines. The better your videos are ranked, the greater chance that a viewer looking online for an attorney will see your video and pick up the phone to call you.

Have you created video today? If not, why not?

See What Your Fellow Lawyers Have to Say About Gerry

"Gerry Oginski is the master of online video."

"Personal injury lawyer and founder of Great Legal Marketing, Ben Glass, says, "Gerry Oginski is the master of online video. If you have not seen his videos, you should. He's done more videos than any lawyer out there. The big edge that Gerry has over his competition is that his videos allow consumers to get to 'know' him before they even pick up the phone. His use of video on his website and his video blog is amazing."

Ben Glass, Esq.
Benjamin W. Glass, III & Assoc., PC
3915 Old Lee Highway, Suite 22-B
Fairfax, VA 22030
703-591-9829
www.BenGlassLaw.com

"Gerry is the leading expert on attorney video marketing... I highly recommend Gerry and his video production services."

"This is Ken Hardison and I'm the founder of PILMMA, the Personal Injury Lawyers Marketing and Management Association designed to help lawyers better market themselves in today's economy.

"I had the pleasure of inviting Gerry Oginski, a New York medical malpractice trial lawyer, to speak at our marketing summit held in North Carolina about video marketing for attorneys. Gerry is the leading expert on attorney video marketing. He has created over 600 educational videos to market his own solo law firm, and is able to compete with the biggest law firms in Manhattan spending millions of dollars per year. How does he do it? By creating videos that potential consumers want to watch. His ideas about creating educational video combined with the latest marketing tools for attorneys makes him stand out from the crowd.

"His videos get noticed. He told a packed room of lawyers from around the country about cases he has obtained, settled and taken to verdict as a result of them hiring him because of his videos. As a result of his remarkable success using video as a highly effective marketing tool, Gerry created the Lawyers' Video Studio to help other lawyers get onto video to market their practices and distinguish themselves from everyone else.

"If you are considering creating video, then you need to contact Gerry Oginski and learn about his Total Online Video Success Program for attorneys. He's not only a seasoned medical malpractice trial lawyer, but he's also an experienced video producer who helps other lawyers create video to market themselves. I highly recommend Gerry and his video production services."

Kenneth L. Hardison
Hardison & Cochran P.L.L.C.
d/b/a Hardison & Associates
4800 Six Forks Rd., Suite 220
Raleigh, NC 27609
919-829-0449
Ken@LawyerNC.com
www.LawyerNC.com

"Gerry Oginski is the leading expert on creating lawyer videos."

Larry Bodine, editor of Lawyers.com and founder of the LawMarketing Channel had this to say: "New York attorney Gerry Oginski is the leading expert on creating lawyer videos. He is the uncontested master of using video to generate new business for lawyers."

Larry Bodine, Editor
LawMarketing Channel
630-942-0977
www.LawMarketing.com

"Having you direct me was a real pleasure. Your relaxed and highly competent manner made me feel I could do my best. You really know what you are doing."

John Burns, Esq.
The Law Offices of John P. Burns
29222 Rancho Viejo Road, Suite 212
San Juan Capistrano, CA 92675
949-496-7000

"I aspire to be the North Carolina version of Gerry Oginski."

"Dear Gerry, It was a truly exciting experience to participate in your Total Online Video Solution [www.LawyersVideoStudio. tv/solutions] and shoot an entire day of video with you and Harry. It invigorates me to be around experts who know what they're doing and who enjoy doing their work with dedication and perfection. It was great to see you again and to learn about what you're doing and how you use the Internet to market your practice. You are a truly amazing person and lawyer. I get worn out simply thinking about all the work you do in a short span of time and all you accomplished simultaneously.

"Your malpractice verdicts and settlements are stunning, particularly in view of the fact that you practice alone. Most big-time malpractice lawyers who I know have a stable of lawyers to take depositions, conduct medical research, prepare written discovery and handle a mountain of other details necessary to successfully prosecute a malpractice case. Your fantastic success in handling complex malpractice cases is especially impressive when you consider that you personally handle your own Internet marketing and also have a separate business. All this and four children still in the home! Thanks."

Brent Adams
Personal Injury Attorney
Brent Adams & Associates
Raleigh, Fayetteville, and Dunn, NC
910-892-8177
www.BrentAdams.com

CHAPTER 24

"Your insight into the typical pitfalls really did open my eyes."

"Gerry, I want to take this time to personally thank you for a terrific hour of time we spent on a personal coaching call. Not only did you 'take it to a new level' in video SEO, but your insight into the typical pitfalls really did open my eyes to what I have been doing wrong that has influenced my results. Thanks again."

Jim Ballidis
Personal Injury Attorney
Allen, Flatt, Ballidis & Leslie
4400 MacArthur Blvd., Suite 370
Newport Beach, CA 92660
888-752-7474

"Many thanks for your coaching!"

"Gerry, I can't thank you enough for guiding me through what would have been a disaster had anyone but you been behind the camera. My PowerPoint slides somehow disappeared from my laptop when using the hotel wireless Internet... or maybe it was my 'fat finger.' In any event, I knew the stuff because I had been giving public seminars on the content for years. But I tend to freeze without a visual cue. So, without visual cues, the day could well have been a huge disaster. While my practice niche is Elder Law, not PI or MedMal, you were like a football or basketball coach; despite my usual stumbles without visual cues, you were successful in getting me to go beyond the stumbles to a successful video shoot. Many thanks for your coaching!"

Richard Habiger
Elder Law Attorney
2010 West Woodriver Drive, Suite 100
Carbondale, IL 62901
618-549-4529

CHAPTER 24

"If I were a law firm looking to add online videos to my website, I would call Gerry Oginski and pay him to come conduct a seminar."

Mike Acosta, a video production manager in Florida, had this to say:

"I had the pleasure of speaking last week with the 'innovator' of online video use for attorneys, Mr. Gerry Oginski in New York. Attorneys need to learn to use online video, as a client conversion tool and educational tool to convert more website visitors into calling clients.

"For any of you who have been living under a rock, Gerry Oginski is the person many of us in the online videos and white-label video platform world consider solely responsible for the movement by law firms to use online videos on their websites. Gerry started doing this years ago when everybody thought it was too difficult, time consuming and required a huge investment and that professionally produced online video was too costly to adapt.

"Gerry single handedly has changed the way attorneys are viewed by their website visitors. You see, Gerry 'gets it.' He decided that instead of using online videos on his website to pitch his firm's expertise and how he can handle your case, he decided it was better to educate his website visitors about the questions they have, prior to calling an attorney.

"Remember, calling an attorney is still a very 'scary thought' for most people, so that is why they research your website first. On www.Oginski-Law.com his library of legal educational tips is the perfect example of how successful the online video market for attorneys can be. His educational video tips allow anyone to see Gerry's personality, his genuine concern for his clients and how passionate he is as an attorney, hell-bent on helping any of his clients *win their case!*

"A quick glance on www.Compete.com shows www.Oginski-Law.com monthly website traffic is up a staggering +37.23 percent and his yearly website traffic is up +59.38 percent in just one year's time! Ask yourself and your law firm's marketing team, 'What do I have to do to get these kind of monthly and yearly website traffic increases from our firm's website?'

"You're going to have to do it with online video, from your website and by using online video networks like YouTube, to drive traffic from YouTube back to your firm's website.

"And, if you want to learn how to do it, you should bookmark www.Oginski-Law.com, because after I spoke to Gerry last week while compiling some information for our monthly Law Firm Video marketing newsletter, Gerry Oginski is on the verge of doing something that will turn the law firm online video market upside down over the next 12 months... stay tuned to www.Oginski-Law.com.

"Here's some really bad news: if you're a New York attorney trying to compete with Gerry, you are about two years behind and well over 200 videos late to the game!

"If I were a law firm looking to add online videos to my website, I would call Gerry Oginski and pay him to come conduct a seminar about how to use online video as a law firm marketing tool. His expertise in the field is invaluable to any law firm looking to tap the greatest marketing tool ever to be used by law firms: online videos."

Mike Acosta is a viral video channel consultant with www.HBProductionGroup.com, a white-label video platform software application that has helped them launch over 100 online viral video channels for website integration into many company websites. His expertise in the areas of affordable online video production services with a packaged video platform can be seen at www.PowerTVOnline.com.

"

"I highly recommend Gerry's services to any lawyer."

Mark Merenda, CEO of SmartMarketing for attorneys, says:

"My clients love the fact that he's a lawyer and not just some wedding photographer with a video camera.

"Gerry's videos are great! Aside from turning out technically superb pictures, he understands the legal marketing field, the right questions to ask, and the concerns attorneys have about their professional image. That means his subjects relax and convey an authenticity that could never be achieved by reading from a script. I highly recommend Gerry's services to any lawyer who wants to create an instant bond with potential clients."

Mark Merenda
CEO
SmartMarketing
3033 Riviera Drive, Suite 103
Naples, FL 34103
239-403-7755
www.SmartMarketingNow.com

"

"You are the man!!!"

"Gerry, We were so happy to finally meet *you!!* We thought that we knew a thing or two about using video in our law practice until we discovered *you.* You are the man!!! Meeting you last week prompted us to completely rethink our video strategy *and* we decided that we weren't doing nearly enough!!! You light a fire under our butts! We are now back in Seattle and refocusing and redoubling our video marketing efforts!!!

"Thanks Gerry!!!"

Mischelle Davis
Client Relations Manager
Davis Law Group, P.S.
Personal Injury Trial Lawyer
2101 Fourth Avenue, Suite 630
Seattle, WA 98121
206-727-4000
www.InjuryTrialLawyer.com

CHAPTER 24

"Educational marketing through video is the future. Gerry is your teacher."

Susan Cartier Liebel, creator of Solo Practice University, says,

"Gerry has the aptitude and technical savvy to create compelling, engaging and highly professional videos to get potential clients to pick up the phone. Educational marketing through video is the future. Gerry is your teacher."

Susan Cartier Liebel, Esq.
Solo Practice University
www.SoloPracticeUniversity.com

"Gerry is really a master of Internet marketing and an authority on effective lawyer video marketing."

"Gerry is really a master of Internet marketing and an authority on effective lawyer video marketing. I highly recommend Gerry if you're interested in custom law firm video to *successfully build your practice.*"

Debra Feinberg
Owner
GetNewYorkLawyers.com
888-529-4696

"We are huge fans of Gerry Oginski."

"We are huge fans of Gerry Oginski at VideoBlogMarketing.com, and here are the top three reasons why:

"3. Gerry's professional and natural presence on video—Gerry is real and you can feel his pure enthusiasm.

"2. Gerry is coaching attorneys to move into this decade! No offense, attorneys, but sometimes you are a bit behind the times when it comes to your Internet presence—listen to Gerry, he knows what's up.

"And the #1 reason Video Blog Marketing is a huge fan of Gerry Oginski:

"1. He sends inspiring and fun emails, keeping us informed, that bring a splash of joy to our day. Thank you Gerry from me, Mary Cary at Video Blog Marketing in San Francisco!

"Keep up the great work, Gerry!"

Mary Cary
Website/Blog Design,
Internet Marketing, Video Production
Video Blog Marketing
415-690-7112
www.VideoBlogMarketing.com

"Online video is the future of law firm marketing and Gerry has more knowledge about that area than any other person."

"Whether trying to learn valuable tips on how to shoot online video for yourself or knowing what to ask an online video company, Gerry Oginski and the Lawyers' Video Studio has quickly become the hub for information about online videos for the legal profession. Online video is the future of law firm marketing and Gerry has more knowledge about that area than any other person. Gerry has become a leading expert about online videos for attorneys and his information has encouraged our firm to increase our use of online video and make it the priority for our marketing and advertising campaign."

Damon T. Duncan
Attorney at Law
Duncan Law, PLLC
628 Green Valley Rd., Suite 304
Greensboro, NC 27408
336-856-1234
DamonDuncan@DuncanLawOnline.com
www.DuncanLawOnline.com

CHAPTER 24

"Gerry is the best-known resource for video for lawyers on the Internet."

Victor J. Medina, Esq.
Trusts and Estates Attorney
Founder of Macs in the Law Office Seminar,
and Macs in the Law Office Podcast
Pennington, NJ

"Gerry Oginski is a master of online-video marketing for lawyers."

"Gerry Oginski is a master of online-video marketing for lawyers. He creates excellent video and is a valuable source of information. But don't take my word for this—view Gerry's videos and judge for yourself. You won't be disappointed."

Jeremy Richey, Esq.
1505 18th Street, Suite #2
Charleston, IL 61920
217-348-6767
JR@JeremyRichey.com
www.JeremyRichey.com

CHAPTER 24

"We will be working to encourage UK law firms to utilize these techniques."

"Gerry, your videos show that you are a tremendous proponent of what to say and how to say it. You understand what your prospective clients are looking for and you take away the FUD (fear, uncertainty and doubt) by answering the questions that your potential clients are using the web to find out about. The content is informative, relaxed and very professional. I am sure your PI business is booming!

"We will be working to encourage UK law firms to utilize these techniques to market their services as opposed to the normal law firm websites which are very introspective and boring. Excellent stuff."

Rod Mitchell
Director
Horsetiger Limited
Managing, Marketing, and Media
25 Campbell Road
Edinburgh EH12 6DT
Scotland
+44 0131-514-6400
Rod.Mitchell@Horsetiger.co.uk
www.Horsetiger.co.uk

"Gerry Oginski is the guru about Internet video marketing for lawyers."

"Gerry Oginski is *the* guru about Internet video marketing for lawyers. His approach of educating lawyers to provide clients, potential clients, and the general public with the content they need when they need it—and to do so in an engaging way that connects the attorney with the viewer—is helping attorneys communicate in the most effective manner possible. Don't believe me that Gerry's video services and consultation is the industry leader? All you have to do is look at who his clients are. They are a virtual 'who's who' of the leading Internet legal marketers. Whenever I have a question or idea about using video for my practice, Gerry is the first person I contact."

Ross A. Jurewitz
Jurewitz Law Group
625 Broadway, Suite 815
San Diego, CA 92101
619-233-5020
www.Jurewitz.com
Blogs: www.SanDiegoInjuryLawyerBlog.com,
www.SanDiegoCarAccidentLawyerBlog.com

CHAPTER 24

"Your videos [are] an example of what the ideal legal video should be!"

Here's a great note I received from Tanner Jones at Consultwebs.com after listening to my presentation at a Lawyer Marketing Seminar (PILMMA) in North Carolina:

"Gerry, Our team thoroughly enjoyed your presentation while in North Carolina. You have obviously mastered the technique and have done a superb job at marketing your law firm via online video. We have all read and enjoyed your book, "How Really Smart Lawyers Are Using Video on the Web to Get More Cases." I have already encouraged a prospective client to browse through your site and view your videos as an example of what the ideal legal video should be."

Tanner Jones
Marketing Consultant
Consultwebs.com
800-872-6590

> *"Gerry… has figured out how to achieve top placement on Google and consistently outrank the big firms."*

"After hearing so much about Gerry Oginski's video work, I was excited to learn he would be presenting at the June Great Legal Marketing Super Conference and most eager to hear him speak. I was expecting a presentation on the technical side of shooting video, such as lighting, camera placement etc. That is stuff I knew from being self-taught, but was interested in Gerry's input on these topics. Surprise—he didn't talk about that stuff at all, other than to say he was not going to talk about the technical side of video shooting. Instead, what we got was far, far more powerful. Gerry, a solo practitioner, has figured out how to achieve top placement on Google and consistently outrank the big firms spending hundreds of thousands of dollars trying to do the same. More importantly he has figured out how to ensure that the people looking for legal help through the Internet find him and get their specific questions answered. The logical next step is for them to call Gerry, the guy who had the answer to their questions and answered them for free without a sales pitch. I joined Gerry's video coaching group the day I got back home."

Gary M. Hazelton
Hazelton Injury Attorneys
677 Anne St., Suite B
Bemidji, MN 56601
218-444-4529
GaryH@1888consult.info
www.HazeltonInjuryAttorneys.com

"I felt inspired after hearing you talk."

I received this great comment from Yvette and Alex Valencia, experts at creating content for attorneys. Here's what they had to say after hearing me speak at Ben Glass' Great Legal Marketing super conference in Virginia in June 2010:

"Gerry, I watched your videos on LinkedIn and Foster Web Marketing's website; however, I didn't think your presentation would be as funny, inspiring and informative as it was. A pleasant surprise! You are super passionate about what you do and it's infectious. I was especially appreciative that you were so willing to discuss your marketing successes. You stole the show! You were witty, well-prepared, and consistent. I felt inspired after hearing you talk.

"You made video seem fun and simple. It's a way to laugh at yourself and allow for others to see you as a person and not just a company. Your success gave us the push we needed to take action.

"After listening to your presentation, we began outlining topics for our company's videos and immediately created a YouTube page. Like you, we understand the value of content. We also understand that by educating our potential clients you can more easily win their trust and hopefully their business. Nowadays content is your sales person and you've got to be out there. Videos can be the next big thing to meeting in person. Thanks so much!"

Alex Valencia
Director of Sales
We Do Web Content
150 SE 12th Street, Suite 301
Fort Lauderdale, FL 33316
888-521-3880
Alex@WeDoWebContent.com
www.WeDoWebContent.com

Now Why Would You Want to Create Video?

COMMUNICATION IS KEY; STAND OUT FROM THE CROWD

You're an attorney. You're a solo. You're a partner in a small law firm of one to five lawyers. You're a marketing executive in a midsize law firm. Maybe you're a partner in a big law firm and attending a seminar and learned about how video can make you come to life and be different than your colleagues.

I know *why* you want to create video. Know how I know?

I'm just like you. I'm a practicing attorney and know exactly what you're going through. How do I know?

I've been in your shoes.

You've tried other types of marketing. You've tried the yellow pages, radio, TV, classifieds, billboards, newspaper ads, networking, and more. You've gone to seminars. But your case intake is down. Calls to your office are down. Your revenue is down compared to last year.

Your accountant tells you the bare-naked truth. You need more clients and cases. Your spouse tells you the same thing. You're a good lawyer and well respected in your field. Yet you're seeing a worrisome trend. You're not as busy as you used to be.

You notice you have more free time and don't understand why. Your profit margin has decreased. Your net income is fluctuating precariously. You go home at night wondering where your next case is going to come from. You're working hard, but the results are not encouraging.

YOU'VE READ ARTICLES ABOUT VIDEO MARKETING

You read an article in your local bar association journal about the benefits of video. You read another article in *Trial* magazine or maybe the ABA's *Law Practice Magazine* about the benefits of video marketing. Maybe you read a book about how really smart lawyers are using video to market their law firms online.

You read some articles at Law.com, Lawyerist.com, TechnoLawyer.com, and LawyersVideoStudio.com about the benefits of video marketing for attorneys. You've gone to legal marketing seminars and heard some thin guy with glasses and thinning hair explain how he used video successfully to market his solo law firm in New York.

You heard him tell you how he has created over 600 videos to market his firm and how he gets calls and emails every day from people who watch his videos.

You learned that this same guy had a free webinar that educated you about video marketing, and you actually took the time to sit in and learn.

You found out this guy has gotten some great results from clients he took in after they watched his videos. Hundreds of thousands and millions of dollars. You listened to video testimonials from other lawyers who took this guy's advice about video marketing. You even went so far as to call a few of those lawyers to find out what they knew that you didn't.

You liked what you heard. You want to do the same.

You have content your viewers want and need. You believe that video is a great way to communicate. You recognize that video is a portal through which you can tell your ideal clients and consumers about how you can help solve their problems. That's why you want to create video.

Want to know who that thin guy with glasses and thinning hair is?

The one who wrote hundreds and hundreds of articles about video marketing for lawyers. The one who wrote the book "How Really Smart Lawyers Are Using Video to Get More Cases." The one who wrote this book, "Secrets of Lawyer Video Marketing in the Age of YouTube." The same one who lectures to lawyers across the country to help them use video to market their law firms. The same one who still is a practicing New York medical malpractice trial lawyer. The same one who founded the Lawyers' Video Studio to help lawyers create entire video libraries to market their law firms.

This is the same guy who has four kids and a great wife who works much harder than he does. Who is this guy?

You know who I am. You've been reading my blog posts and articles for years. You've been watching my videos just as long. You've heard me at seminars. You've seen the testimonials from other really smart lawyers and from well-known legal marketing experts. You've seen the social proof and you've done your homework and due diligence.

YOU WANT VIDEO FOR YOUR LAW FIRM

There's an easy way to get it.

Do it yourself or hire a video marketing company to do it for you. I can't tell you which one to choose. I can, however, make a suggestion.

- Are you the type of person who fixes a broken sink, or do you call a plumber?

- Are you the type of person who fixes a hole in your roof, or do you call a roofing specialist?

- When your car breaks down, do you put your car on blocks and fix it in your driveway, or do you take it to your local mechanic?

- If you need appendix surgery, do you go to the library and learn how to do the surgery yourself, or do you go to the best surgeon you can find?

Well, counselor, you've reached the end of this book. I have a question for you. Are you a little closer to the type of person who likes to do it yourself or are you a little closer to the type of person who prefers to have an expert do it all for you?

I know which I'm closer to. Which one are you closer to?

If you are closer to the attorney who wants it all done for you, then you need to reach out to my production manager and send an email to Kathleen@LawyersVideoStudio.com and let her know you'd like to chat. Or pick up the phone and call Kathleen at 800-320-4314.

If you are closer to the lawyer who wants to do it yourself, then I have a treat for you. I'm creating an online video training program for the do-it-yourself attorney that is available online at LawyersVideoStudio.com.

SCAN WITH YOUR SMARTPHONE
TO WATCH & LISTEN TO A FREE ONLINE
VIDEO TRAINING PROGRAM FOR THE
DO-IT-YOURSELF ATTORNEY.

You've Reached the End... But Your Journey Just Begins

Before you leave, I want to thank you for taking the time to read my book. Since you've taken the time to learn about video marketing and how it can help you, I want to invest in you. I want to give you a special opportunity and a challenge.

This special opportunity is a chance to learn how to create video on your own for $25,000 off my standard pricing. No joke.

The challenge is to commit and make a decision to create video, right now. It doesn't matter whether you create video on your own or hire an experienced video company to create video for you. You need to make a decision. Successful attorneys are able to make decisions. Really successful attorneys learn how to implement those decisions. As my good friend and mentor Kevin Nations says, "Imperfect action is always better than inaction."

You owe it to yourself. You invested the time and resources to learn how to take your marketing to the next level. You are clearly on the right track. You recognize how important video marketing is for you and your law firm.

My challenge is for you to commit to a plan that will allow you to create video. Once you make that commitment, you establish an obligation to yourself, to your family and your law firm. That obligation will help you grow and open your eyes to an entirely new world of video marketing.

FOR THE DO-IT-YOURSELF ATTORNEY

For lawyers who consider themselves to be do-it-yourselfers, like me, my introduction video tutorial program may be the perfect program for you. You get to see exactly what I have done to successfully market my law firm in the most competitive market in the country. You will have the ability to ethically copy and model what I do in order to create video on your own.

If you want to learn how to create video on your own, my video tutorial program allows you to watch exactly what I do to create my videos. I take you behind the scenes. I show you step-by-step exactly how I come up with my content, my ideas and compelling headlines to get viewers interested in my videos.

My video tutorial program allows you to see the planning and production, editing and publishing phases that happen when I create my videos.

To learn more about my innovative $25,000 off video program, head over to http://everythingiknow.lawyersvideostudio.tv.

FOR LAWYERS WHO WANT A DONE-FOR-YOU VIDEO MARKETING PROGRAM

For those lawyers who do not have the time, desire or energy to create video on their own, then I have another great opportunity for you. You have the ability, if you are the ideal client for me, to participate in my Total Online Video program where I help you create at least 50 videos in a one-day video shoot. If you think you are the right attorney for me, I encourage you to call my production manager Kathleen at 1-800-320-4314 to set up a phone consultation with me. You can also e-mail her: Kathleen@lawyersvideostudio.com. I welcome your call.

SCAN WITH YOUR SMARTPHONE TO WATCH & LISTEN TO A FREE ONLINE VIDEO TRAINING PROGRAM FOR THE DO-IT-YOURSELF ATTORNEY.

Learn About Gerry

Gerry is known as "America's leading authority on video marketing for lawyers." He is a practicing medical malpractice trial lawyer in New York and has created a video marketing solutions company called the Lawyers' Video Studio to help lawyers market their law firms online. In fact, he is the only practicing trial lawyer in the country who helps other lawyers create video to market their practice.

Gerry has written hundreds of articles about video marketing for lawyers, created over 600 educational videos to market his law firm successfully, and lectured across the country on the subject of video marketing. He loves helping lawyers transform their marketing from dull, boring, and ineffective messages into educational and compelling videos that show why they have information that potential clients need to know.

GERRY OGINSKI, ESQ.

Founder, Lawyers' Video Studio
Chairman of the Board, Lawyers Video Marketing Alliance

25 Great Neck Rd., Ste. 4

Great Neck, NY 11021

800-320-4314

Gerry@LawyersVideoStudio.com

LawyersVideoStudio.com

WA